W9-DCY-835

OF COURSE YOU'RE

YOU'RE

Also available from Harper/Hazelden

Fat Is a Family Affair, Hollis
Keeping Promises: The Challenge of a Sober Parent, Porterfield
Of Course You're Angry, Rosellini and Worden
A Parent's Survival Guide: How to Cope When Your Kid Is Using Drugs, Hodgson
The Twelve Steps of Alcoholics Anonymous, Hazelden
Raising Drug-Free Kids in a Drug-Filled World, Perkins and McMurtrie-Perkins
Young, Sober & Free, Marshall
When a Bough Breaks: Mending the Family Tree, Nilsen
Codependent No More, Beattie

The Hazelden Meditation Series

Twenty-Four Hours a Day
The Promise of a New Day: A Book of Daily Meditations
Each Day a New Beginning: Daily Meditations for Women
Today's Gift: Daily Meditations for Families
Night Light: A Book of Nighttime Meditations
Touchstones: A Book of Daily Meditations for Men
Day by Day: Daily Meditations for Young Adults
Food for Thought: Daily Meditations for Dieters and Overeaters
The Love Book
Days of Healing, Days of Joy: Daily Meditations for Adult Children
One More Day: Daily Meditations for People with Chronic Illness

OF COURSE YOU'RE

ANGRY

by Gayle Rosellini and Mark Worden

WARNER MEMORIAL LIBRARY
EASTERN COLLEGE
ST. DAVIDS, PA. 19087

A Harper/Hazelden Book

Harper & Row, Publishers, San Francisco

New York, Cambridge, Philadelphia, St. Louis
London, Singapore, Sydney, Tokyo, Toronto

2-3-95

HV 5132 .R67 1986
Rosellini, Gayle
Of course you're angry

OF COURSE YOU'RE ANGRY. Copyright ©1985 by the Hazelden Foundation. This edition
published by Harper & Row, Publishers, Inc., by arrangement with the Hazelden
Foundation.

All rights reserved. Printed in the United States of America. No part of this book may
be used or reproduced in any manner whatsoever without written permission except in
the case of brief quotations embodied in critical articles and reviews. For information
address Harper & Row, Publishers, Inc., 10 East 53rd Street, New York, NY 10022.
Published simultaneously in Canada by Fitzhenry & Whiteside, Limited, Toronto.

FIRST HARPER & ROW EDITION PUBLISHED IN 1986.

Library of Congress Cataloging-in-Publication Data

Rosellini, Gayle.
    Of course you're angry / by Gayle Rosellini and Mark Word-
en.—San Francisco : Harper/Hazelden, 1985.
    96 p. ; 22 cm.
    ISBN 0-06-255442-5 (pbk.)

    1. Alcoholics—Family relationships.   2. Anger.   3. Alcoholics—Psycholo-
gy.   I. Worden, Mark.   II. Title.   III. Title: Of course you are angry.
HV5132.R67   1985   362.2'92—dcl9   86-45385
                         AACR 2   MARC

90   91   92   FG   10   9   8   7   6

CONTENTS

CHAPTER ONE
Anger and Recovery

It's after midnight and Donna is furious. She wonders for the hundredth time why she puts up with it. Does anyone really need this torture? Why isn't her husband, Jim, home yet? He left for his Alcoholics Anonymous meeting at quarter to eight, and five hours later he's still gone! The damn meeting only lasts an hour and a half. Where *is* he? If he's drunk again . . . .

No, don't even think it, she warns herself. It's been a year, Jim's been sober a year. He wouldn't, he couldn't.

Where is he?

Crouched into a corner of the sofa, Donna is in pain, an agony of fear, worry, and resentment. Wasn't Jim's getting sober supposed to make everything better? Wasn't it supposed to be the start of a bright new life, a life unmarred by the turmoil and arguments of the old drinking days? Hadn't she gone to all those meetings and read all those books just like the counselor recommended? Hadn't she accepted the fact that alcoholism is a family disease, that, in her own way, she'd been just as sick as Jim? Hadn't she done her share, for God's sake, to patch together the shreds of a marriage slashed to pieces by alcoholism?

Where *is* Jim? If sobriety is so wonderful, why is their marriage still awful, why the pounding heart, the clenched jaws, the aching, crushing pressure in her chest every time Jim pulls another one of these stunts? Doesn't he know what it does to her? No. She'd married a man too insensitive, too self-centered — he'd never understand the depth of her fury.

What was wrong with her, anyway? Why did she feel so much hatred? Why did she feel so *much*?

Baffled, Donna looks down into the black, bitter dregs of her coffee. *Very appropriate,* she thinks. Then she tries to shake off her venomous thoughts. Jim is sober, that's the important thing to remember. She must concentrate on that. Sobriety comes first. That's what the counselors always say. Sobriety is the *most* important thing.

Jim is sober, but nothing else has changed. Jim's out doing his thing while she sits home, sick with worry. *Nothing has changed*. The memory of all those terrible nights stabs at her heart. Why didn't she just get a divorce and be done with it? Jim doesn't care. Oh, he pretends to care but all he *really* cares about is himself. Otherwise, he wouldn't treat her this way, would he? Would he?

But what can she do about it? She certainly can't let Jim know how she feels because if she does, if she loses control of her temper for one minute, everything will come pouring out — a roaring flood of anger, a torrent of pain, a relentless upwelling of savage and ugly resentment. And then it will be too late. Because once she starts, she might not be able to stop, and it'll all come out, all of it. She'll be shattered by the pent-up fury of her soul. She might start screaming and never be able to stop. And then Jim might drink again.

The glare of headlights flashes in the window. Jim is home.

She greets him at the door, her bravely smiling face hiding her anger, masking the inner turmoil. "Hi, honey," she says with a strained voice. "You're late." The smile on her trembling lips hardens.

"You didn't have to wait up," he says defensively. "Some of the guys and I went to the coffee shop after the meeting. Guess I lost track of the time."

"Oh, well . . . . " A shrug, a pretense of indifference. Jim bends to kiss her. Clamping her mouth tight, she turns her cheek to his lips, sniffs, inhales deeply. Cigarettes and coffee and stale Old Spice. Safe, friendly smells. No alcohol. A sigh of relief escapes Donna's lips.

Jim stiffens. "For crying out loud," he complains, a sour smile twisting his mouth. "What did you expect?"

She turns away. "I'm going to bed," she says. "I'm tired."

"Wait." He grabs her arm. "I want to talk."

Shaking loose, she whines, "If you want to talk, go back to your friends at Denny's." Her voice is low, almost soft.

Jim's eyes narrow. Sighing, he says, "You wanted me to quit drinking and I did. Now, you're mad because I go to meetings. I can't win."

"I'm not mad." Her voice is flat, her jaw tight. "I'm just tired."

"Yeah, tired. You're always tired." They glare at each other in silence for a moment before Jim turns and heads for the bedroom. As he walks away, he says just loud enough for Donna to hear, "One of these nights I may not come home at all." He slams the bedroom door behind him.

Donna stands staring into space, an empty feeling in her stomach. *We're getting better,* she commends herself, a tear rolling down her cheek. *Neither one of us lost our temper. Maybe things will work out after all.*

Everyone gets angry, feels — to one degree or another — the arousal of resentment, the turmoil of rage, the heart-thumping seething of fury. We feel irked, exasperated, irritated, vexed, annoyed, enraged. We don't always like to admit it, but all of us get angry at one time or another.

Anger is a normal human emotion. To never feel anger is to never be fully human. Yet intense, uncontrolled anger can hurt and destroy, wreaking havoc and pain. Anger — angry people — can kill.

How many spouses have been beaten, children battered and abused, loved ones murdered in a terrible storm of savage anger? A cruel blow, once delivered, can never be taken back. All the tearful apologies and gifts given as peace offerings can't erase the pain of physical and verbal punches delivered in anger. Uncontrolled anger can leave permanent marks.

What to do then? Swallow our anger? Put on a brave, smiling face like Donna? Deny the anger exists and hope it will go away?

When pushed down and hidden, anger can be like slow-acting acid splashed on our self-esteem. It gnaws, eats, burns, corrodes until nothing is left but a raw-edged hole, an empty pit of despair. Sometimes, suicide looks like the only way out. So what, my recovering friend, does any of this have to do with *you*? You haven't murdered anyone and you haven't committed suicide — at least not lately. Sure, you get a little ticked off once in a while. Piqued, perhaps. But ever since you got sober (or your spouse, or your kid, or your parent got sober) things have been a lot better. Really! Honest! It's just that sometimes, well . . . .

This is a book about anger, specifically about anger and the process of recovery from alcoholism and other forms of chemical dependency. And that's what all of this has to do with you. With us. Because we're not going to find an angrier person in the world than an alcoholic, unless, of course, we look at the spouse and kids of an alcoholic. And getting sober doesn't make all that anger magically disappear.

Sometimes sobriety makes anger worse, for the family anyway. At least when the alcoholic is drinking, we have something to blame the anger on. The bottle. The booze. The drunkenness. We can hate the *alcohol,* we can detest the *alcoholism*, and somehow still manage to love the alcoholic. Take away the drinking or other drug use and what do we have left? All that anger with nothing to blame it on! And that doesn't feel good.

We end up confused.

Weren't all the awful family problems supposed to stop once Dad got sober? Well, he's sober now, but the house is still filled with tension. He doesn't kick in the door and break the dishes anymore. He doesn't launch into drunken tirades like he used to. He doesn't stay out all night and leave us wakeful and terrified that the phone might ring, with a gentle official voice regretfully informing us Dad was in a fatal accident at 2:00 A.M.

So, it is better. There's a small sense of trust developing, slowly, almost as if we're cordial strangers. But there's tension in the air, mixed with the memories of all of yesterday's pain. You see, when an alcoholic first sobers up, there isn't much of a change in the family dynamics. The situation — and the anger — in the family is still far from normal, far from healthy.

We're supposed to be happy now, but the pain and anger don't magically disappear. We still have work to do. Sobriety, in and of itself, is no guarantee for happiness. For an alcoholic, it's the starting point, the single most important thing necessary to begin the *process* of recovery.

The *process*.

Remember that. *Recovery is a process.* Sometimes dramatic changes happen in a blinding flash of insight, a sudden and surprising awakening in our minds. Most of the time, it's a slow and painstaking thing, a snail-like crawl to growth, maturity, and happiness.

And the process takes work.

Learning to deal effectively with anger is part of the process, not only for the alcoholic, but for the spouse and children (even grown, adult children) of the addict. Each of us must go through our own recovery process, because chemical dependency doesn't hurt just the addict. It hurts the family, too.

This book isn't just for the person recovering from alcoholism or another form of chemical dependency. It's for the man or woman who loves or at one time loved a chemically dependent person. It's for the son or daughter of an alcoholic, the mother or father of an addict. It's for all of us.

We have special problems with anger. In alcoholic families, anger is often expressed in extreme ways, through violence, emotional abuse, and neglect, or through abandonment. We become afraid of anger; when we express it, we may be overwhelmed by feelings of guilt. Fear, anger, guilt; for us these emotions are all tied together in a negative way.

Because we're afraid of anger, we say, "Well, the drinking has stopped, so let's put all the bad things away and forget they ever happened." We try to ignore our angry feelings, hoping all the time they'll go away. But they don't. They usually get worse. Then we feel guilty because we're thinking such venomous thoughts and feeling so vicious. And when that happens, we end up behaving in ways that can hurt us and the people we care about.

We have special problems with fear, anger, and guilt.

Our goal is learning to accept angry feelings as normal. We want to learn to deal with anger without fear and guilt. Most importantly, we don't want our anger to hurt us or other people.

An important note: This book won't help a *drinking* alcoholic. First, we have to get sober. This means giving up pills and pot as well as booze.

RULE #1 FOR ALCOHOLICS AND OTHER ADDICTS
Sobriety first, then emotional fine-tuning.

Recovery for those of us who love or live with an alcoholic does *not* depend on that person's sobriety. It helps if the addict gets straight — it helps if the alcoholic quits drinking, but we can begin our own recovery even if that person continues to drink. And even if the chemical dependency continues.

Learning to deal with our anger and resentments, learning to forgive people who have hurt us, and learning to forgive ourselves for the wrongs we have committed can be the most important elements of our own recovery.

Remember: Anger is a normal emotion. Normal emotions don't have to be eliminated. Whether we admit it or not, we all sometimes feel angry. Recovering people are no exception. If we've dulled our emotions with alcohol and other drugs for years, feelings of anger during recovery can frighten us.

Like Donna in the preceding story, we might be afraid of the intensity of our emotions, afraid it will destroy us and our family. We're also afraid of rocking the boat. If we express our anger it might spur the chemically dependent person to go on another binge, so we clamp our mouths shut and hope for the best.

Though Jim is sober and both he and Donna have participated in counseling, they still have big problems in their marriage. Communication problems. Anger problems. They don't yell and scream and kick at each other, but the anger is there in the clenched jaws, the rejected kiss, the cold stares, the slammed doors, the subtle threats.

Unresolved anger, whether it is openly discussed or not, can hinder the recovery process.

Some anger is fragmented and white-hot, loud, explosive, frightening. We recognize that kind of anger. We can see it and hear it and feel it. But there's another kind of rage: controlled, quiet, polite, ice-cold. This kind of anger often lives in families where a chemically dependent person has sobered up, but neither the addict nor the family is working on the recovery process.

For positive recovery to take place, this anger needs to be acknowledged, dealt with, and resolved. We need to know there are healthy ways to express anger, that the management of anger can contribute a great deal to the *process* of recovery, making it less stressful and reducing the chance of relapse.

A caution or two before we begin: There's no "quick fix" for any problem with human emotions. There's no wizard who's going to come along and plink us on the head with a magic wand and, once and for all, make us okay. And there's no drug that will make anger go away and leave us alert, fully-functioning human beings.

More than anything, we must be willing to look closely at sensitive areas of our lives, to learn, and to risk and be open to change. We must be willing to work.

We also must realize that we have a natural aversion to dealing with these problems. Why? Because it can be painful! But, then, chemical dependency *is* painful. It would be a great mistake to ignore where we have come from in our attempt to determine where we are going. The pain of recovery is nothing compared to the pain of addiction.

Of course, before we decide to take the risks and do the work needed, we have to decide if we want the things that learning to deal with our anger can help us discover. Do we, by any chance, want:

To love and be loved by our families?
To like ourselves?
To reduce *much* of our anxiety?
To enjoy sex?
To become more healthy physically and mentally?
To enjoy our work more?
To have more caring friendships?

To be less depressed?

To learn to forgive those who have injured us and to earn forgiveness for the wrongs we have committed?

Okay, if we want these things, then possibly this book might help, but here's another test. Since this book is for people who want to learn to deal better with anger, we have to find out if anger is interfering with our recovery process. Answer true or false to the following statements. Please, be honest. Not "lip-service honest," but fearlessly and searchingly honest. Fourth Step honest.

1. I don't show my anger about everything that makes me mad, but when I do — look out!
2. I still get angry when I think of the bad things people did to me in the past.
3. Waiting in line or waiting for other people really annoys me.
4. I fly off the handle easily.
5. I often find myself having heated arguments with the people who are closest to me.
6. I sometimes lie awake at night and think about the things that upset me during the day.
7. When someone says or does something that upsets me, I don't usually say anything at the time, but later I spend a lot of time thinking up cutting replies I could and should have made.
8. I find it very hard to forgive someone who has done me wrong.
9. I get angry with myself when I lose control of my emotions.
10. People really irritate me when they don't behave the way they should, or when they act like they don't have the good sense God gave lettuce.
11. If I get really upset about something, I have a tendency to feel sick later, either with a weak spell, headache, upset stomach, or diarrhea.
12. People I've trusted have often let me down, leaving me feeling angry or betrayed.

13. When things don't go my way, I get depressed.
14. I am apt to take frustration so badly that I cannot put it out of my mind.
15. I've been so angry at times I couldn't remember things I said or did.
16. After arguing with someone, I hate myself.
17. I've had trouble on the job because of my temper.
18. When riled up, I often blurt out things I later regret saying.
19. Some people are afraid of my bad temper.
20. When I get angry, frustrated, or hurt, I comfort myself by eating or using alcohol or other drugs.
21. When someone hurts or frustrates me, I want to get even.
22. I've gotten so angry at times, that I've become physically violent, hitting other people or breaking things.
23. At times, I've felt angry enough to kill.
24. Sometimes I feel so hurt and alone I feel like committing suicide.
25. I'm a really angry person, and I know I need help learning to control my temper and angry feelings because it's already caused me a lot of problems.

If you answered true to ten or more of these statements, you are seriously prone to anger problems. It's time for a change.

If you answered true to five questions, you are about average in your angry feelings, but learning some anger management techniques can make you a happier person.

If you answered true to even one of the last four questions, then your anger has reached a danger level! Perhaps we can help you get your anger under control before it takes your life out of control. Shall we begin?

CHAPTER TWO

In the Beginning, The Family Created Anger

For most of us, the crux of our anger recovery plan — our plan to acknowledge, accept, and cope with our angry and aggressive feelings — is that old standby, *knowledge.* Insight, motivation, and behavior-change spring from knowledge. But let's face it, no matter how much knowledge we have, we will probably never attain total serenity.

And it's probably a good thing we won't. A nation of totally blissful citizens might never have the gumption to get anything done. But even though we might not become totally serene, we can become happier than we are now. To do that, we have to learn how to make positive changes in ourselves wherever we possibly can. We also have to learn to accept the fact that some things can't be changed. The hard part, as the Serenity Prayer suggests, is learning the difference between the cans and the can'ts.

Some Can'ts

We can't change anybody but ourselves.
We can't change the past.
We can't always get our own way.
We can't always make people do what we want them to do.

Some Cans

We can change ourselves.
We can change our future.
We can change how we feel when we don't get our way.
We can change how we act when people don't do what we want them to do.

We can also learn to understand our anger, what sets it off, and how to live with it. It's important for us to know that anger is not some unpredictable and unknowable beast hunkering down inside us, waiting for our defenses to crack, our armor to crumble, our will to weaken so it can lunge out like a roaring monster grabbing control of our mouths and hands and hearts. Anger doesn't have to be bad.

Anger is a commonplace human emotion. It is not mysterious, but as psychologist Carol Tavris points out, anger is very frequently *misunderstood*. The strain of misunderstood anger can make recovery rockier than it need be. Worse, the uncontrolled expression of anger can lead to bigger problems such as job loss, child abuse, spouse beating, and troubles with the law. It can also lead back to the bottle.

LOOK: We're not saying anger causes chemical dependency. But we do know that the anger we feel and our responses to other people who are angry with us can have a lot to do with individual and family recovery.

Here's a bit of knowledge that might help us better understand anger: Much of our anger starts in the family, continues in the family, and stubbornly refuses to go away even if we leave our families.

Anger and the Alcoholic Family

Families are a little like Mount Everest. They make us angry because they're there. "Marriage and family living generate in normal people more anger than people experience in any other social situation," says marriage counselor David Mace. Notice Mace is speaking about normal people and normal anger.

One of the reasons we feel angrier with loved ones or friends is because we feel safer and more secure in their company. We have a pretty good idea of how they will respond to us. But there are other reasons:

Close contact provides more opportunities for anger to develop.

Irritations can become cumulative.

We are inclined to try to get loved ones to change, and we get angry when they don't.

Loved ones are inclined to try to get us to change, and we get angry when they try.

Now, if this is true of *normal*, happy families, it's quite reasonable to expect that anger problems will be worse in dysfunctional, chemically dependent families.

All families with an alcoholic member possess at least one thing in common — unpredictability.

Depending on the drinker's level of intoxication and mood, family life can vary from a hilariously happy party atmosphere to one of intolerable brutality — all in the same hour. Anxiety, tension, and fear lurk constantly in the air, even on the best days.

The alcoholic family, with its unpredictability and ill-defined or nonexistent family roles may breed helplessness, shame, neglect, insecurity, and mistrust. It also breeds anger.

What causes the most anger problems in recovering alcoholic families? It's the past, things that happened last year, five years ago, fifteen years ago. We recall with burning resentment every injustice, every offense, every wrong committed against us. Never mind if the injury is remembered through an 80 proof filter; the memory is embedded deep and it festers.

Stockpiling resentments is a skill refined to a high art by many alcoholics. But it isn't the exclusive property of those recovering from their own chemical dependency. Family members — spouses and children — know a thing or two about carrying a grudge.

Let's face it: We're all hiding wounds that haven't been allowed to heal, *resentment wounds* — the gashes, trauma, and lacerations of bitter anger. Our resentment wounds can very often have a bad affect on our jobs, marriages, and friendships. And, of course, our recovery.

Living in an alcoholic family is painful. Every member of the family lives with uncertainty, fear of emotional or physical abuse, anxiety over their own well-being and for the safety of their loved ones, anger over their feelings of powerlessness, and constant chronic disappointment. Psychiatrist George Vaillant has compared living in an alcoholic family with being an inmate in a concentration camp. Dr. Timmen Cermak says people who grow up in a chemically dependent family often suffer from post-traumatic stress syndrome.

The pain is real, the trauma is real, the anger is real. But there's nothing we can do to change the past. All we can change is the way we allow the past to affect us now. And we can't change the people who hurt us either. The only person we have the power to change is ourselves. Luckily, when we change, the good effect often rubs off on the people closest to us.

All Members of an Alcoholic Family Suffer

We've all heard the phrase *alcoholism is a family disease.* The words roll easily off the tongue, and for those of us who have been in treatment for alcoholism or other chemical dependency, the words lapse into a meaningless slogan, almost like a stock greeting card cliche. *How's it going? Have a happy day. Alcoholism is a family disease.*

Stop and think about it. What do we mean when we say alcoholism is a family disease?

First, we have to understand that alcoholism and other chemical dependencies are actual physiological disorders that can have severe medical complications. In fact, there is abundant scientific evidence that a predisposition toward alcoholism can be inherited. In other words, if you have a close blood relative who is alcoholic, and *if you drink,* you may run a higher than normal risk of developing alcohol problems yourself.

There's more. If you have a close blood relative who is alcoholic, you may also inherit a predisposition toward depression. Here's the tricky part. Even though alcoholism is a physical disease and people don't become alcoholics on purpose any more than diabetics purposely develop diabetes, family members face archaic taboos about alcoholism that make us feel ashamed and guilty about living in an alcoholic family, or even admitting to ourselves that someone we care about is alcoholic. The alcoholic denial system teaches us to hide our feelings of grief, guilt, and anger.

So we cover up. We pretend the problem doesn't exist. We put on a good front and try to conduct our day-to-day lives as if every little thing is just fine and dandy, when in reality our lives are chaotic, inconsistent, and filled with anxiety, embarrassment, and dread.

The taboo against alcoholism acts as a pathetic a[...] form of social control which delays the drinker an[...] members from seeking the help so desperately nee[...] to recover. What happens in the family is this: Nobody talks about *IT*. Nobody talks about the disease of chemical dependency, the bad feelings, the unpredictability, the fear. It's as if everyone in the family — the addict, the spouse, the kids — is engaged in a giant conspiracy of silence about the one thing that needs to be brought out into the open: the chemical dependency.

Oh, to be sure, there's a lot of talk and blame and recriminations skirting *around* the issue, but everyone is so busy protecting and blaming and covering up that no real progress is ever made. Unfortunately, this very same process can continue after the chemically dependent family member sobers up. The destructive patterns — the conspiracy of silence — become embedded, almost habitual, as family members grope in desperation for healthy responses to an unhealthy situation.

It's this conspiracy that affects the nonaddicted members of the family. That's why we call it the family disease. Everyone, not just the drinker, is affected. The result? Feelings of frustration, blame, powerlessness, confusion, self-pity, alienation, distrust, and an absolute sense of aloneness in a hostile world. We learn to hide our real feelings, and we learn distorted and unhealthy ways of expressing them.

We're angry, but we don't know how to deal with it! And guess what? The majority of alcoholics and other drug abusers suffered from the family disease long before they took their first drink or popped their first pill. They had an alcoholic parent or grandparent.

So, is it any wonder that people who live in alcoholic families have anger problems? The fact that we suffer from angry feelings doesn't make us strange or bad people. We have no reason to be ashamed or guilty about our feelings. After what we've been through, it would be amazing if we didn't emerge with more than our share of unresolved conflicts.

Anger is one of the symptoms of the family disease, and it is a symptom that lasts long after the drinking has stopped. Learning to cope with anger is an important part of the recovery process. But we have to remember not all anger looks alike and it's not always readily recognized. It can take many forms — violence, depression, manipulation, compulsive eating, vandalism, suicide, and so on. These varied responses can mask what's really going on under the surface: fulminating rage.

Let's stop and check your knowledge and attitudes for a moment. Answer these questions with a yes or no.

1. Do you accept anger as a normal and commonplace human emotion?

2. Do you think learning to understand, accept, and cope with your angry feelings is an important part of your personal recovery plan?

3. Are you beginning to accept the idea that living in an alcoholic family breeds angry feelings?

4. Are you willing to believe you have no reason to feel guilty or ashamed of your feelings?

5. Can you see that angry feelings can continue even after sobriety, or after you no longer live with an addict?

6. Do you understand that anger can be expressed in many ways, some of which might not look like anger on the surface?

If you can answer yes to these questions, congratulations! You've already gained some knowledge about anger and you're developing more healthy attitudes about your feelings. If you can't honestly say yes to all six questions yet, don't despair.

Try this instead: Go back and review what you've read. Think about it. Talk about it with a friend. Talk about it with someone who has also lived in an alcoholic family. Compare notes.

And remember: We can't become instant anger experts. There's still a lot to learn! Let's start by looking at some different temperament styles.

CHAPTER THREE
Anger Styles

Lynn, 35-years-old and six months sober, clearly remembers her mother's frustration over Lynn's bursts of adolescent temper. Infuriated, her mother would shout, "You'd better learn to control that temper of yours, young lady, or you're heading for big trouble!"

What was the "big trouble"? In Lynn's home, "big trouble" was never clearly defined. It could have meant anything from a sharp reprimand to a thump on the side of the head with a two-by-four.

But Lynn got the message. Because her mother's temper was bigger, louder, and more practiced than her own, Lynn soon learned to lower her voice and watch her language. That strategy satisfied Lynn's mother, but it didn't help Lynn very much.

"I was still mad," Lynn recalls. "I hadn't learned to control my temper, I'd learned to *stifle* my temper, to sit on it. Inside, I was still boiling, and sometimes I even got physically ill — with nausea and stomach cramps — from my pent-up anger. But I couldn't admit it, not even to myself. I was well brought-up, which meant I had to pretend, I had to act."

It wasn't difficult. All Lynn had to do was act pleasant and unruffled, as if she were capable of handling any situation without getting upset.

"I should have gotten an Academy Award for my Nice Girl performance," Lynn says ruefully. "After all, Nice Girls didn't have ugly emotions, and I was a Nice Girl, wasn't I?"

Does Lynn's story sound familar? In many families, young girls learn to be passive and well-behaved on the surface. Underneath, they seethe. But they learn to deny the unpleasant emotions. They learn that Nice Girls don't have Bad Emotions. They learn the fine art of denial.

Lynn's home was a breeding ground of denial, and the behavior patterns carried over to adulthood.

"I still have trouble expressing my anger," Lynn reveals. "I'm still a 'nice girl.' If my husband does something that makes me mad, instead of telling him how I feel, I'll pretend it doesn't bother me. If he pushes me, I'll fib a little. I'll say, 'I'm not angry. I'm hurt.' Then sometimes I'll cry."

Why does Lynn hide her real feelings from her husband, the one person in the world she wants to be closest to? Part of it is her "nice girl" conditioning and part of it is fear — fear of losing control, fear of being rejected and abandoned, fear of making a fool of herself, fear of her own emotional intensity.

She explains it this way, "Usually, I don't show my feelings about things that make me mad. I used to drink and take tranquilizers when I was upset about something. I kept a placid surface. But now that I'm sober, now that I'm drug-free, I find myself exploding at odd times and it scares me. It might be a little thing that sets me off, but it's like a volcano erupting. All this anger and bitterness spews out. My husband and kids are stunned. I scream at them, I call them names, I tell them how they're taking me for granted and I can't stand it any longer. Then they yell back at me and everyone is hurt and angry and upset, and it's all my fault. I just hate myself afterwards. I feel guilty and stupid and selfish."

Lynn is trying to learn better ways of conveying her feelings to her family, and for good reason. When she swallows her anger, pretending it doesn't exist, and when she explodes, overreacting to a minor irritant, Lynn starts craving a drink again. For Lynn, anger management is an essential part of her recovery plan.

Girls aren't the only ones in our society who are taught to hide their true emotions. Boys, too, are conditioned to express their feelings in certain distinctive ways. At an early age they learn to deny their emotions, especially feelings of tenderness or weakness. But young men are allowed feelings of anger and aggression, they're even encouraged to cultivate them. "Stand up for your rights," they are urged. "Don't take any guff!" "Don't let anyone push you around!" "Win!" "Be a man, and for God's sake, don't cry!"

Perhaps this explains why some men will react with an outburst of temper when they are confronted with a situation which makes them feel sad, embarrassed, or frightened.

When Lynn experienced feelings of fury, she said, "I'm not angry, I'm hurt." She lied to her husband and to herself about what was going on inside her. Men do the same thing. "Hell, no, I'm not scared," they'll say, "It doesn't bother me."

There's not one ounce of evidence that men, as a group, are any angrier than women, or vice versa. But it doesn't take a controlled scientific study to tell us men are more overtly aggressive about expressing anger and rage. For proof, all we have to do is look at the violent crime statistics. Males far outnumber females as perpetrators of violence. Violence often stems from rage.

So does depression. Women, turning their anger inward, refusing to even acknowledge the feeling exists, suffer from depression much more often than men. They take more psychotropic medication (drugs that act on the mind) and are hospitalized more often for depressive illness. These sex-role differences, however, tend to get blurred. They aren't sharply drawn; they aren't universal. We all know outspoken women who can rival any man in bellowing and belligerence. Similarly, we know soft-spoken men who are nurturing and mild-mannered.

The point is this: We learn how to express our emotions (all our emotions, not just anger) at an early age. We learn in our families. We watch our parents and our brothers and sisters and we imitate or rebel against them. We are rewarded for certain behaviors and punished for others. And the rewards are often arbitrary and inconsistent. All the time we're learning and feeling.

Although emotions — love, fear, anger, joy — are innate in all of us, the interpretation and expression of those emotions is learned in our families. We all *feel,* but we don't all *show* those feelings in the same way.

Feeling emotion and expressing emotion are two distinct

things. Feeling is innate. Expressing is learned. We don't all show our feelings in the same way.

The Spock Syndrome: Born Vulcan

Sometimes when I'm doing therapy with chemically dependent people and their families, I ask this question: If you could be any popular real or fictional character, whom would you choose to be like?

One person regularly receives about 80 percent of the votes. My clients, male and female, say if they could be anyone, they'd want to be Mr. Spock.

Do you remember Mr. Spock, the half human, half Vulcan of *Star Trek* fame? When insulted by Dr. McCoy, when frustrated by balky antimatter devices, when under attack by hordes of nasty Klingons, Spock coolly raises an eyebrow and murmurs, "Fascinating."

While Captain Kirk seethes, gyrates, agonizes, emotes, and sweats, Spock merely observes the situation, checks his computers, applies the proper logical solution, and saves the Enterprise for one more voyage. Although Kirk is every bit as heroic as Spock, and certainly more human and humane, never once have I had a client tell me they'd like to be Captain Kirk.

You see, Captain Kirk is so . . . well, *emotional*. He hurts, he suffers, he yells, he even cries. Unlike Spock, Kirk *feels*.

But don't we all?

To my way of thinking, Kirk is a much better emotional role model than Spock, simply because he is so human, he feels so much, and he expresses those feelings without trampling other people. When his basic emotions (we *all* have them) — vengeance, hostility, aggression, rage — thunder to the surface, he struggles with them, he acknowledges them, and he rises above them. Of course, the process is painful. Much of life is.

Perhaps that's why so many of my clients admire Spock's emotional style. Spock is above pain, above anger, above the embarrassingly sloppy emotions we humans are heir to. If we could be like Spock, we would be spared all the pain of being human!

We would be stolid, stoic, and unflappable. We would have the essence of courage — grace under pressure. But, try as we might, none of us will ever be able to duplicate Spock's emotional style. We're not hewed from granite or marble; we have no green Vulcan blood in our veins. We're stuck with the *human* condition.

How much better it is to admire Kirk with all his emotional weaknesses! At times, we all behave in ways we are less than proud of. Each of us possesses weaknesses that can cause our downfall if we're not careful. We behave erratically. When under pressure, we sweat like horses, our fingers tremble, and our stomachs churn. But, like Kirk, we also have strengths to counterbalance these minor imperfections in our character.

We're going to talk about four different emotional styles — four different ways of expressing anger. Almost everyone fits into one of these categories, although it's rare to find a person who is "pure" to type. It's more common to be predominately of one temperament style, with a tinge of one of the other types to spice up the personality.

Once we understand which style best fits us (and those we care about) we can work to eliminate our weak points while developing our strengths.

The Bulldozer

The Bulldozer is always pushing, reaching, succeeding. If a job needs doing, a Bulldozer gets it done. Bulldozers refuse to believe there is anything about them that might need improving, adjusting, or changing, but they can see *your* weaknesses a mile away. Successful executives, athletes, and entertainers are often Bulldozers. So are many mothers. Their motto in life is, "I'm right and you're wrong." They'd be impossible to tolerate if they weren't so darned successful and charming.

STRENGTHS	WEAKNESSES
Leader	Bossy
Forceful	Short-tempered
Outspoken	Rude
Decisive	Controlling

Competitive	Aggressive
Productive	Workaholic
Daring	Insensitive
Convincing	Manipulative
Strong-willed	Stubborn
Firm	Unsympathetic
Independent	Selfish

Strong point: The Bulldozer is a great worker and can accomplish wonders in a short time.

Strong point: The Bulldozer is persistent and is not easily discouraged.

Strong point: Bulldozers are not afraid to stand up for what they believe is right.

Problem: The Bulldozer can be a bully.

Problem: The Bulldozer is insensitive to the needs of others.

Problem: The Bulldozer always has to be right.

Anger Style: Bulldozers can be short-tempered and argumentative. Because they always want to be right, they don't listen to other people's opinions and they disregard their partners' feelings. Bulldozers win arguments, but are often resented and disliked.

Improvement: Learn to listen. Try to accept the idea that other people have a right to be different from you, and just because they are different doesn't mean they are wrong. When talking with another person, practice these statements: "How do you feel about that? What do you think? What's your opinion?"

The Brick

While lacking Mr. Spock's heroism, the Brick comes closest to the Vulcan's emotional flatness. Avoiding conflict, extremes, and excesses, the Brick travels down the middle road, offending no one, doing what is expected, and not asking for attention. Because the Brick doesn't like to make decisions, he or she makes a perfect follower. Bricks make pleasant company and great diplomats. Their motto is, "Don't rock the boat."

STRENGTHS	WEAKNESSES
Agreeable	Compromising
Tactful	Boring
Friendly	Superficial
Obedient	Submissive
Inoffensive	Bland
Listener	Uninvolved
Patient	Indifferent
Contented	Aimless
Forgiving	Fearful
Obliging	Indecisive

Strong point: The Brick is adaptable and can make the best of almost any situation.

Strong point: The Brick is diplomatic and doesn't hurt others' feelings.

Strong point: The Brick can have a dry sense of humor.

Problem: The Brick is wishy-washy.

Problem: The Brick is uncommunicative.

Problem: The Brick is stubbornly boring.

Anger Style: Bricks refuse to talk about their feelings because they fear conflict. Their anger shows up in a chronic lack of enthusiasm for the plans, ideas, and wishes of family and friends. Bricks quietly pour cold water all over another person's excitement, but never come out and say, "No, you can't do that." Since a Brick refuses to make a decision or take responsibility, it's always somebody else's fault if something goes wrong.

Improvement: Learn to talk about feelings and desires. Try to show enthusiasm when someone you care about is excited over a new project, idea, or plan. When talking with another person, practice these statements: "Hey, that's a neat idea! That's really exciting! What I've decided is . . . ."

The Soulful One

The Soulful One is the mind, heart, and spirit of humanity. These people carry the weight of the world on their shoulders. Feeling unique, alienated, and lonely, they find happiness is always just out of their grasp. Natural helpers, Soulful Ones are often embroiled in other people's problems. They lean toward the arts and the helping professions — counseling, teaching, nursing, social work, and motherhood. Their motto is, "Woe is me!"

STRENGTHS	WEAKNESSES
Behaved	Compulsive
Loyal	Insecure
Thoughtful	Moody
Deep Thinker	Depressed
Perfectionist	Critical
Benevolent	Unforgiving
Idealistic	Naive
Sensitive	Thin-skinned
Self-sacrificing	Resentful
Persevering	Vengeful

Strong point: The Soulful One is sympathetic to the plight of the needy.

Strong point: The Soulful One is a giving, caring person.

Strong point: The Soulful One can be counted on when the chips are down.

Problem: The Soulful One is frequently gloomy, depressed, and insecure.

Problem: The Soulful One does not express needs directly.

Problem: The Soulful One puts unreasonable demands on family and friends, and usually ends up disappointed and hurt.

Anger Style: Guilt is the Soulful One's most-used weapon. They try to make the other person feel guilty and apologetic for letting the Soulful One down. Because they are so insecure, they are afraid of alienating the love of family and friends, so they don't express their anger directly. They use hurt looks, sighs, and the cold shoulder. They also direct their anger inward, sometimes becoming compulsive eaters or semi-invalids.

Improvement: Learn to lower your expectations of other people. Try being open and honest about your needs without trying to make other people feel guilty if they can't or won't meet them. When talking with another person, practice these statements: "What I need is . . . . What I want is . . . . I feel angry because . . . ."

The Lightheart

All butterflies and rainbows, the Lightheart is the life of the party, a joy, and a frustration. When things get heavy, these people dance away singing and laughing. Their motto is, "Call me irresponsible." They often skip from job to job, but there's only one occupation that really suits them: Independent wealth.

STRENGTHS	WEAKNESSES
Optimistic	Dreamer
Affectionate	Unfaithful
Persuasive	Talkative
Young-at-heart	Immature
Sociable	Loud
Enthusiastic	Undisciplined
Dramatic	Show-off
Promoter	Con Artist
Spontaneous	Forgetful
Cheerful	Shallow

Strong point: Lighthearts are fun, lively, and popular.

Strong point: Lighthearts make new friends easily.

Strong point: Lighthearts can live by their wits.

Problem: Lighthearts have difficulty developing deep and lasting relationships.

Problem: Lighthearts are insensitive and their wit can turn cruel.

Anger Style: Lighthearts throw tantrums. They pout, stamp their feet, make scenes (best if performed before a large audience), and disappear. Their witty exits leave friends and family laughing until they realize the Lightheart has escaped scot-free and *they* are left holding the bag. Lighthearts shrug off anger quickly, and because they lack empathy, they can't understand why everybody makes such a fuss over their antics.

Improvement: Learn to accept responsibility. Try not to run from problems and negative situations, rather stick with a problem until you have solved it. When talking with another person, practice LISTENING to what *they're* saying instead of to the music of your own voice.

Each of these four emotional styles can result in an interesting and healthy personality. No single style is better than another; all can produce simply marvelous people. All can produce horrors! When taken to an extreme, an emotional style can be downright disabling. Read on, and we'll explain two dangerous ways of expressing anger.

CHAPTER FOUR

When Anger Disables: The Violent Ones

Do you know one of these? They hit first and ask questions later, but they always hit someone smaller and weaker than they are, someone who can't or won't hit back hard enough to really hurt them. They also hit walls and cars, smash windows and dishes, break noses and hearts. Afterwards, they say they're sorry, they didn't mean it. But, almost inevitably, they do it again. And they hate themselves for it.

We're not talking here about hardened criminals, gangsters, muggers, serial killers, or rapists. Career criminals, sociopaths, and the insane may wreak havoc in the streets, but let's face it, those kinds of people don't read self-help books. They don't care who they hurt, but you do.

Most violent people don't hurt strangers. They hurt the people they love — their mates, their children, their elderly parents. Paradoxically, many violent people are well-liked and respected by friends and co-workers. They are often considered pillars of the community. Because their everyday behavior belies the violence simmering under the surface ready to erupt at the slightest provocation, half the people who know them would be stunned by the truth.

They wouldn't believe it unless . . . well, of course, there's only one possible explanation: The victim must have done something really *awful* to deserve such a beating! This twisted logic keeps the violence alive. It's called blaming the victim. It lets the abuser off the hook, keeps the victim quiet, and allows the violence to continue.

Alcoholism and other forms of chemical dependency promote family violence. That is why violence is common in chemically dependent families, and it's not always the drinker who's doing the hitting and breaking. The spouse and children of an addict can be so consumed by frustration and rage that they strike out — a mother abusing her children, a child abusing a pet. Violence can trickle down from the strongest to the weakest member of the family. Dad hits Mom. Mom hits Sissy. Sissy hits baby brother.

People who discover they can get away with ranting and raving, intimidating, hitting, kicking, breaking, and hurting have learned an extreme way of expressing emotion.

Did you know that the most under-reported crime of violence in the United States is spouse abuse? Some studies report that upward of *50 percent* of American women are physically or psychologically abused by their husbands. Much of this abuse stems from impulsive rage reactions promoted by stress and alcohol or other drugs.

Even after sobriety, the violence may continue unless the Violent One learns to channel aggressive feelings in less dangerous ways. Abusers seem to snap — become their most violent — when under pressure. While improving our lives tremendously, sobriety does not guarantee freedom from pressure. It does not give us immunity against rage and violence. Being sober for two years didn't prevent Don C., a 32-year-old truck driver, from snapping. The owner-operator of an eighteen-wheeler, Don was under a great deal of financial stress. Out on the road for days at a time, he slept little and survived on junk food.

The last time he came home, he discovered his wife had gone, taking their seven-year-old daughter with her. For Don, it was a crushing blow. He was confused and frightened. He was jealous and stunned. A capricious set of emotions jerked him around like a puppet on a string.

Don snapped — just like that, he came apart in the middle of a telephone conversation with his counselor. This is the way the counselor recalls it, "Don was very upset when he called, but he seemed to be in control. His wife had walked out. His whole home life had suddenly collapsed, and he was frantic. His conversation grew progressively fragmented, disjointed.

"Finally, Don said, 'I just don't know what to do. Why did — why did she — I can't understand. . . .' There was silence on his end of the line and then I heard him moan, 'Oh, God!' It was a pitiful wail, and then he bellowed like a wounded bull."

The counselor shakes his head in disbelief. "I tell you it made the hair stand up on my arms. It made me shiver. I've never heard anything like it." What happened? The counselor heard the telephone receiver thud to the floor. And then came the sound of breaking furniture, the brittle crash of breaking glass. And in the background Don's heavy breathing rasped loudly. He had been transformed almost instantly into a hurt and enraged beast, inarticulate except for the eerie gutteral wailing that came as he wrecked his house. Finally, the rampage ended. Silence.

"Don? Don?" The counselor called into the telephone. The heavy, labored breathing came closer to the phone. "I'm — I'm sorry," Don apologized. "Something . . . I guess I just snapped."

Don snapped, all right. And that wasn't the first time it had happened. His rampages had been the cause of his wife's departure. As she later explained, "After living for ten years with a Jekyll and Hyde personality, I left. When Don got sober, I thought everything would be better, and for a little while it was. But his unpredictable temper finally drove me away. I never knew what was going to happen. He might come in the door all smiles, but if he didn't like what I fixed for dinner, he'd go into a frenzy, calling me names, breaking things, hitting me. I couldn't take it any longer."

She didn't want to be around Don when he snapped. And she wanted to get her daughter out of harm's way.

Why did Don snap? Probably there's no single reason. However, his behavior typifies a common, and frightening, trait found among the Violent Ones — a bizarre lack of proportion. A burned dinner will evoke a response as intense as the loss of a family. There's no discrimination between a minor irritation and major catastrophe.

Drinking and other drug use, by lowering inhibitions, seem to incite family violence. But Don had successfully dealt with a serious drinking problem. He had stopped drinking. He was dry as the saying goes, but not recovered. If rage reactions continue after we achieve sobriety, we must acknowledge that we are not yet recovered. We need to seek further treatment specifically for our anger problems.

Men aren't alone as abusers. Hot lines all over the country are reporting an increase in calls from *men* who have been beaten by their wives. One woman, infuriated by her husband's late hours and drinking, waited until he fell asleep in their bed, then she tied him up in the sheets and beat the living daylights out of him with a heavy cast-iron skillet. He went to the hospital; she went to jail.

Violent women, however, don't usually target their husbands for abuse. They hit their children. Most child abusers were themselves abused as children. They learned young that "might makes right;" they learned to express their anger and frustration through their fists.

Both men and women abuse children, and older children have been known to hurt younger ones. The cycle goes on and on. Do you see the pattern?

Violent people don't beat up people who are bigger and stronger than they are. Men beat up smaller men, weaker women, and children. Big kids hurt little kids. Women abuse children, and, when furious enough, women get themselves an equalizer in the form of a gun or a cast-iron skillet and attack men when they are made vulnerable by sleep or drunkenness. Even the biggest man crumples when hit with lead.

There's an important message here. People with violent tempers are often described as *uncontrollable*. "I couldn't help it," they rationalize. "I couldn't stop myself." Nonsense.

Only a crazy person would run out into the middle of the street, flag down a Hell's Angels motorcycle gang, and yell, "Hey! I'm mad as hell and I want to fight!"

If the violent expression of anger is truly an uncontrollable and unstoppable urge, why, then, do we let the motorcycle gangs drive merrily by while we wait to get home to clobber the wife or kids?

The answer is simple. Even when we seem gripped by the claws of uncontrollable rage, we're still making lightning quick, *rational* decisions. We're saying to ourselves, "Can I get away with this? How badly will I get hurt if I start hitting? Is it worth the risk? Yes, I think it is." Pow!

And if someone gets hurt? We say grimly, "They had it coming."

We decide to be violent. Yes, yes, we're really doing this! Really thinking these kinds of thoughts, really making a *rational* decision. Unfortunately, these thoughts flash through our heads like meteors on a sunny day. The bright light of our rage and denial blinds us to the process. We don't remember *deciding* to go berserk. We aren't aware that the decision-making process even occurred. But it did!

You don't believe us? Well, when was the last time you took on a motorcyle gang? Or the karate champ of the West Coast? Or the three-hundred-pound gorilla who used to date your wife? See? When necessary, you *can* control your uncontrollable temper.

Now, think about this for a minute: If this rational thinking process is going on in our heads when we're in the throes of intense emotion, if we really can control our tempers when it's in our selfish best interest to do so, just think what a powerful tool this rational thinking process can be if we become aware of it — if we use it, if we learn ways to practice control on a daily basis.

We can learn to control our violence, but we may need help. How do we know when we need more than self-help? Ask yourself these questions:

In the last year. . .

1. *Have you hit, slapped, choked, kicked, punched, bitten, strapped, burned, pushed, shaken, thrown, or beaten another person when you were angry?* The point of this question is, have you *hurt* another person during an argument? And we're not asking how badly you hurt them. That's often a matter of luck. Today's grazing slap can be tomorrow's knockout punch. Or death blow.

2. *Have you abused a child in any of the above ways?* Look, we're not talking about a light swat on the bottom to discipline a child who has run out into the road. But if you spank a child hard enough to leave a bruise, scratch, or welt; if you kick or slap the child; or shake them until their heads rattle, you have an anger problem — one that can permanently harm your child.

3. *When angry, have you on more than one occasion broken dishes or windows, hit walls, torn up clothes, destroyed furniture, thrown objects about, or vandalized your own or someone else's property?* Not all violent people attack other people. Breaking every dish in the house may be better than hitting your child, but it's not a rational way to deal with anger.

4. *Have you killed or purposely injured or tortured an animal because you were angry?* Cats and puppies are frequent targets of misplaced anger, especially with young people.

5. *Have you waved a gun or club or knife at someone when you were angry?* We don't mean a burglar here. Grabbing a weapon when you're angry is extremely dangerous, and even if you don't intend to do anything more than scare the person, there's no guarantee that someone won't be hurt accidently.

6. *Have you been involved in a traffic accident because your anger affected your driving?* A car can be a deadly weapon, too, often with innocent bystanders as the victims.

If you answered yes to even one of these questions, you are one of the Violent Ones. Can you do anything about it? Most certainly! However, and this is a *big* however, you probably can't do it on your own. You need professional help.

Getting the Right Kind of Help

If you are alcoholic or chemically dependent, and not already a member of Alcoholics Anonymous or Narcotics Anonymous, the time to join is right now. A.A. or N.A. can do more than simply dry you out. These self-help groups can help you reach *full* recovery in the very best way. Not by magic or by feel-good pills, but by working a recovery program with other folks who care, one day at a time. A.A. is in the phone book, and it's free.

You will feel welcome and comfortable the moment you walk in the door. So don't delay.

You may also need to become involved in individual or group therapy. But beware. You need therapy that will deal *directly* with your specific problems of anger and violence. This means you may have to shop around to find the right therapist.

Traditional Freudian psychoanalysis, involving several sessions a week over a period of years, is *not* recommended in your case. You need treatment that will intervene in your violent behavior NOW! You don't have time to explore your childhood in search of some hypothetical "real" underlying cause of your behavior. You need to change now.

Look for these things in a therapist:

- Knowledge and experience in treating alcoholism and other chemical dependency — as primary illnesses, not as symptoms of some other psychological ailment. (Therapists who do not understand alcoholism can do you more harm than good.)
- An emphasis on cognitive, behavioral, or rational-emotive therapy. (This type of therapy deals with the "here and now" and works to change your attitudes and behavior.)
- A therapist who does *not* recommend the use of tranquilizers or other mood-altering medications. There is no evidence that medication works with extremely angry or violence-prone people. (Alcoholics and other drug abusers should be extremely wary of mood-altering medications. For us, it's no different than drinking!)

Do you need a psychiatrist, that is, someone with a medical degree? Not necessarily. A psychologist, or social worker, or counselor can be just as effective.

How do you find a therapist? This is sometimes difficult. You can ask your family doctor for a recommendation, or you can call your local mental health center. Many hospitals are now offering psychological services. One of the best ways is to ask your friends. Have they seen a therapist who has been effective in helping them improve their lives?

While seeking out a therapist, don't be shy. You have every right to question them about their background, training, philosophy, methods, and fees before you sign up for a course of counseling.

And don't be coy. Tell the counselor right up front, "I'm an alcoholic. I have an anger problem. I beat my wife." It may be embarrassing to admit, but you must tell the truth if you want to change. So here's a chance to be honest about your faults in a safe place, where the object is not to punish, but to help. And remember: Counselors are not mind readers. *You* have to tell them what you think your problem is. The counselor may uncover other problems you aren't aware of, but don't waste time playing guessing games. The counselor might not ask the right questions. It's your job to honestly reveal your problems.

What if you are a child abuser? Some states require counselors to report all confessions of child abuse to the authorities. Please don't let this prevent you from getting help. Your child's well-being, even his or her life, may depend on your having enough courage to face this problem head-on.

If there is a child abuse hot line in your area, call them and ask for help. You won't have to give your name.

Getting Help for the Victim

What if you are not the Violent One? What if you're the victim of someone else's violence? You need help, too. You probably feel frightened, guilty, and alone. Please, now is the time to reach out for help!

There are several things you can do. First, if there is a Battered Persons' Shelter or Help Group in your area, call them. You *don't* have to move out of your home and into a shelter to receive advice and counseling from these groups. They can offer you moral support and guidance; they can give you acceptance and understanding. These things are crucial as you make your first faltering steps out of your victim's role.

Here's another suggestion that works. The next time you are the victim of violence, call the police and *press charges*.

Recently, an experiment in Minneapolis showed that if the violent person (usually a husband, stepfather, or boyfriend) in a family disturbance is arrested and removed from the home, even for a few hours, the chances of future family violence are dramatically decreased.

It didn't matter whether or not the offender was *convicted* of the assault or disorderly conduct charges. What *did* matter was that the Violent One learned that if he started hitting, he had to pay the consequences. If he knows he can't hit you and get away with it, he'll think twice before he knocks you around again. So, call the police! Scream bloody murder. Don't allow yourself to be the victim. You don't deserve to be beaten!

And that brings us to another point. Victims of violence often feel guilty, as if they deserve to be abused and unfortunately, our society often reinforces this view. Many women, suffering from low self-esteem and dependency upon the man who beats them, feel they have no other choice but to take the violence. Don't you believe it!

You have the right to live without the fear of violence. Don't let anyone tell you you must like getting beaten up or you wouldn't stay. Hogwash!

You may need professional help to raise your self-esteem, reduce your dependency, and muster the gumption to stand up for your rights. Don't wait for the Violent One in your life to make the first move toward recovery. It's up to you! Get help now. All you have to lose are your bruises.

CHAPTER FIVE

When Anger Disables: Nice People

Do you know anyone who is self-sacrificing, considerate, idealistic, and sensitive? Loyal and faithful — someone you can always count on? Certainly not one of those selfish types always seeking to be the center of attention, always clamoring, "Me, me, me." Someone who's considerate, thoughtful, willing to share.

An ideal person, right? Someone you'd like to be around, the perfect mother and wife, the perfect friend. Or perhaps, the perfect martyr.

Not all angry people express their anger with bellows and blows and malevolent housewrecking. Nice People (N-Ps, for short) swallow their anger, smiling as the bitter potion scalds their tongues. Swallowing anger doesn't make it go away, it just makes your stomach hurt.

Of course, not all idealistic, sensitive, loyal people are simmering cauldrons of unexpressed anger. Many are healthy, happy, assertive, and sincere folks who are exactly what they appear to be on the surface: nice people.

Happy Nice People and angry N-Ps are alike in an important, superficial way — they're well-behaved, socialized, mannerly. So, when an N-P gets angry and stays angry, she can also seem well-behaved. On the surface, anyway. But underneath, hidden from view, a chronically angry N-P harbors feelings that can lead to trouble. They are fussy and thin-skinned, moody and resentful, insecure and withdrawn, critical and hard-to-please, unforgiving and vengeful, depressed and shy. But on the surface, *they're nice.* They work hard to keep their negative feelings — their real feelings — hidden.

Feeling unworthy and inadequate, and fearing rejection if anyone should find out what they're *really* like, the chronically angry N-Ps put on a good front for the world while stewing with fear and resentment on the inside.

Nice People attempt to bolster their shaky self-esteem by "helping" people. N-Ps can't do enough for other people. They work hard, giving of their time, energy, and money. They have special sympathy for underdogs, and often involve themselves with people who are depressed or suffering misfortune.

This may sound highly admirable, but in the context of the alcoholic family it can be as dangerous as dynamite. Why? Because the only way N-Ps can maintain any feeling of self-worth is by associating themselves with someone who is sick or weak or more troubled than they are. In other words, N-Ps lose their sense of worth when the other person — say, the alcoholic spouse or troubled child — is no longer weak, sick, or confused. Without someone to "help," to be better than, N-Ps feel worthless.

Alcoholics and N-Ps form secret (unspoken) pacts with each other. He will drink a lot. She will lecture him about the drinking, cover up for him, keep the creditors away from the door, and hide the problems from the rest of the family. He gets to keep drinking; in fact, he even uses her nagging as an excuse for drinking. She gets to think of herself as a moral, superior person for putting up with this inferior drinker; plus she gets the admiration of other people for "holding the family together." Substitute "addict" for "alcoholic" in the description above and the same pattern holds true for other forms of chemical dependency.

Why does an N-P behave this way? Why do we sabotage the people we love?

Anthony Storr points out in his book, *Human Aggression*, that Nice People like us feel fundamentally unlovable, and thus, our sympathetic nature — our niceness — is merely superficial. We hunger desperately for love, yet we are frightened of appearing assertive or aggressive in any way, afraid we will be rejected if we openly ask other people to care for us or meet our needs. Storr says we will submerge our own personality in that of the other person, and will use our capacity for doing this as a kind of emotional blackmail. Our excessive concern over the other person's feelings is a childish maneuver to gain love, power, and a sense of self-worth. We will destroy the people we love before we allow them to be healthy, free, and independent!

What we're talking about here is another extreme of anger disability. Just as the Violent Ones learned to get away with mayhem, N-Ps learned they couldn't. N-Ps express anger through passivity, guilt-tripping, manipulation, and self-destruction.

An agreeable and pleasant demeanor can hide aggressive and hostile feelings. Passive people can be just as angry as violent people.

N-Ps can be of either sex, but Nice Women seem to outnumber Nice Men. Nice Women are common in alcoholic families. The person most likely to be a Nice Woman is one who grew up with an alcoholic parent. Often, she marries an alcoholic. She may appear to be outwardly independent, but essentially she is a dependent person. She has an unusual capacity for putting herself in another person's shoes, for showing sympathy, for taking care of the needs of others. She is a friend in need, a natural caregiver who is often embroiled in the crises of others.

She's also frequently depressed, overweight, and manipulative. She has seriously considered suicide more than once. While her husband turns to the booze bottle, the N-P frequently turns to the medicine chest, becoming hooked on prescription pain pills, diet pills, or nerve pills.

What she wants most in the world is to be loved. But she's never learned how to say, "Hey, dammit, love me!" Plus, she's never learned to *accept* the words "I love you" when she hears them because she feels so basically unlovable. No matter how much attention and love she is given it's never enough, never the right kind, never satisfying. Happiness is always a few inches out of her grasp. She is a casualty of the disease of chemical dependency.

The daughters and wives of alcoholics often express their anger through dependency, self-sacrifice, manipulation, and self-destructive behavior.

On the surface, N-Ps are generally regarded as unusually kind people. They are able to sympathize with others and share their feelings. But their niceness, their self-sacrificial tendencies, can turn ultimately disagreeable.

As a typical N-P, I will give you the shirt off my back, then criticize you (for your own good) for not wearing the shirt with style. And because I went naked for your benefit, I caught a chill and ended up with pneumonia. "But don't worry," I say (cough cough), "you (with your giant wardrobe) needed the shirt more than I."

Do you see the pattern here? Our seemingly selfless acts of giving provide us with a power base, a base from which we can criticize, control, and punish. The recipient of our good will is, of course, obligated to return the favors by bestowing attention, affection, and blind loyalty upon the self-sacrificing N-P.

But people being what they are, the recipient of all this generosity is often ungrateful. Worse: They can be downright selfish, mean, and awful! Does this mean the N-P has failed? Not in the least! Because, you see, only a despicable coward would mistreat a person as giving, as considerate, as thoughtful, and as *nice* as the N-P.

The N-P wins again. Their low self-esteem is bolstered by the attention of those obligated to them, or by the knowledge that they are morally superior to the ungrateful dog who has used them, then mistreated them.

N-Ps use gift-giving, guilt, and manipulation to control other people. Sadly, these manuevers ultimately backfire. Those people the N-P seeks to bind to her, to make dependent, and to control, end up resenting and often rejecting her. And although feelings of moral superiority can give us a temporary lift, they can't keep us warm at night. N-Ps seek love and approval. They want other people to validate their self-worth because they don't know how to do it for themselves.

They want control. Yes, control! Because they *fear* what they cannot control. They fear abandonment and reflection. Often that's what they get.

Why? Because, as Anthony Storr says, it is hard for anyone to love and respect someone who hardly exists in her own right. And while the N-P's selfless acts may be appreciated temporarily, she can become intensely irritating because the gifts she gives are never without strings. The target of all the gifts pays, and pays dearly, with guilt and anxiety and unhealthy dependence.

The N-P rarely makes direct demands on family and friends. Instead, they drop hints, manipulate, sink into silence, display their pain, and withdraw their affection. It's as if they're saying *I'm suffering and it's your fault*, but they won't say it out loud, right up front, where people can deal with it.

The result? Family and friends feel angry and guilty while grudgingly trying to give us what they think we want. We feel angry and hurt and demeaned because we *know* they don't *really* care about our feelings. Everyone loses.

Okay, this may not be a very healthy or honest way to deal with anger, but is it really disabling? The answer is a resounding YES! This quiet kind of anger can actually be more destructive and difficult to deal with than outright violence. Let's look at some of the ways Nice People are disabled.

1. *N-Ps are terrible money managers.* We spend so much money on gifts and "special treats" for friends and relatives, we often have to borrow money to meet our own basic financial obligations. If we are being fully or partially supported by another person, we may express our anger by running up huge bills for our mate to pay.

2. *Many N-Ps suffer from an eating disorder.* Unable to express our feelings directly, we turn to food for solace. It would not be inaccurate to say that behind every smiling fat lady is an angry lady struggling to get out. Overeating can be a way of quietly rebelling against critical and demanding parents or spouses. However, our obesity often affects our self-esteem negatively.

3. *Many N-Ps develop chronic physical ailments that prevent them from fully participating in family life or employment.* Angry N-Ps usually suffer from one or more of the

41

following chronic disorders: obesity, heart trouble, ulcers, severe headaches, intractable pain (often back pain), adult onset diabetes, weak spells, diarrhea or constipation, colitis, sleep disorders, and general nervousness. Sometimes there is no specific ailment, just a general malaise that defies medical diagnosis. Because we are so busy taking care of other people, we don't have time to take care of ourselves. We often shun doctors; or conversely, are frequently hospitalized, often for surgery.

4. *N-Ps are frequently depressed.* Depression is common among alcoholics, and it is also common among their children. Medical researchers believe some (or much) of this depression is biochemical in nature and related to heredity. However, in N-Ps this depression can be related to our feeling so unlovable and worthless, compounded by the disappointment we feel when friends and family don't meet our (unspoken) needs.

5. *It's not unusual for N-Ps to have sex problems.* Although angry, an N-P is too passive to tell a sex partner, "I don't want to have sex with you because I'm angry, riled, and upset over . . . ." Women may show a total lack of interest in sex, or may punish a partner by willingly (even eagerly) engaging in sex, then showing no pleasurable responses. This can be a way of saying, "See how inadequate you are. You can't turn me on."

In a man, anger may be manifested through lack of interest in sex or the refusal to ejaculate during intercourse. "I'll show you who's in control," he seems to say. His basic message is similar to the angry woman's. Of course, there are many other reasons for sexual dysfunction, but anger cannot be ignored as a possibility.

Extramarital affairs or excessive promiscuity can also be a sign of anger against spouses, parents, or other authority figures. If this sexual activity brings little pleasure, lots of guilt, or if the sexual partner is merely a faceless blur, it's a dangerous sign.

6. *N-Ps sometimes threaten suicide or make suicide attempts to frighten their friends and loved ones.* These attempts are framed in a "See what you made me do" mind-set. In teenagers and young adults, females make 90% of the suicide attempts, but account for only 20% of suicide deaths. These failed attempts may be a way of punishing and manipulating family and friends or an attempt to gain sympathy.

Although the N-P may not really want to die, these suicide threats and attempts must be taken seriously because a fake attempt can go disasterously wrong, ending in death or serious disability. An N-P with a history of failed suicide attempts may also decide to go for the real thing while in the depths of a depression.

7. *N-Ps can turn violent.* It may sound contradictory for an N-P to also be a Violent One, but it's not uncommon. N-Ps have such a compulsive need to control, to get their own way, that their frustration can reach intolerable levels. Their human targets are almost always small children who are dependent on the N-P for care and survival. During adolescence, when the child is old enough to reject the N-P through running away, withdrawal of affection, or turning to another adult for help, the physical abuse usually stops. N-Ps are also known for temper tantrums during which they break dishes, shatter glasses, throw things, and rip up clothes.

If you recognize yourself in even one of these seven self-destructive behaviors, you may be an angry Nice Person. If you see yourself in two or more, especially, if you've ever attempted suicide or turned violent, you are suffering from an anger disabilty.

Can you be helped? Yes, of course! But you *will* need help.

Getting the Right Kind of Help

If you are a nonaddicted codependent and not in Al-Anon, why not? Al-Anon can help you deal with your guilt and fear and with your need to control. Al-Anon is listed in the phone book. Its members are women and men who love an alcoholic and who are struggling to find peace and happiness. They know what you're going through.

Besides self-help, you may also want to seek professional individual or group psychotherapy. But listen, N-Ps are very resistant to therapy. We're so *good* at meeting the needs of others, so nice, so skilled at submerging our own personalities into those of other people that we can easily end up *giving therapy to our therapists*!

Listen some more. This is a very serious problem for us. Our therapists and the other group members may think we're absolutely wonderful — so nice, so giving, you know — but we don't get any help for our problems! Our ability to deflect confrontation by "helping" the other group members and by being so attentive and supportive of our therapists *hinders our own recovery*.

So, if you go into therapy, you must be brutally honest with yourself and your therapist. You might even take this book with you and point to this page and say, "I have this problem!" Forewarned is forearmed. If your therapist knows in advance that you are an N-P, you have a better chance of getting help.

Because N-Ps are so insecure and suffer from low self-esteem and passive-aggressive behavior, we can especially benefit from assertiveness training and other groups that help us become more direct in stating our needs. Women N-Ps can blossom beautifully in women's support groups that are nurturing while working to build self-esteem and feelings of independence.

If you are overweight and suffering from compulsive eating, the last thing you need to do is go on a diet. You've probably already done that a hundred times. What you can do is join an organization that will help you understand your eating disorder, such as Overeaters Anonymous.

Is your health bad? Are you depressed? More importantly, are you engaging in destructive and addictive habits? Do you smoke like a smokestack? Eat junk food and sugar by the ton? Never exercise? Are you using prescription tranquilizers, pain pills, or sleeping pills? How about over-the-counter diet aids, laxatives, nerve pills, or sleeping pills?

Many of the health problems plaguing N-Ps are life-style problems and can be drastically improved with good nutrition and exercise. An important note: Many people also report an improved mental outlook when they improve their nutrition and life-style.

Dealing With an N-P You Love

A.A. can help alcoholics learn to deal with sabotaging N-Ps and Al-Anon can help nonaddicted codependents. The best way to avoid an N-P's sabotaging behavior is to learn to say no, gracefully, to any attempts to take care of us. If we continue to accept money and gifts, if we allow an N-P to lift the load of our responsibilities from our shoulders, we are heading straight for trouble in the form of guilt, anxiety, anger, and relapse.

Detaching ourselves from the grasp of an N-P can be difficult and painful — for us and them. If you are the adult child of an alcoholic — for example, if your father was an alcoholic and your mother an N-P — you would be doing yourself a big favor by getting in touch with the National Association for Children of Alcoholics. NACoA addresses the concerns of women and men who are still suffering the aftereffects of growing up with an alcoholic parent. Adult children of alcoholics don't recover simply by leaving home. The wounds of the disease of alcoholism can last a lifetime if they are forever hidden from the healing powers of the open air and sunshine of understanding and acceptance.

There are also Al-Anon groups that focus on adult children of alcoholics, and there are a growing number of Adult Children of Alcoholics (ACoA) self-help groups springing up in communities across the country. These groups are a valuable resource for those who still feel confused and emotionally upset by the experience of growing up in a family affected by one of the addictions.

CHAPTER SIX

Resentments

Resentment is defined as anger and ill will caused by a real or imagined wrong or injury. The dictionary gives the word *hatred* as a synonym for resentment. Sometimes I think resentment is like a pet rattlesnake. Half the time it just lays there, kind of lazy and quiet and inconspicuous. Then, whammo! Something stirs it up — a noise, a movement, a threat. Then the snake lithely coils, hisses, and strikes. The fangs sink in deep, the venom flows into the victim's bloodstream to sicken and kill.

The main difference is that when we get resentful, we strike and fang ourselves, and the poison that runs through our veins is of our own making.

Unreasonable resentments are a hallmark of the family disease of alcoholism. And recovery cannot occur unless we learn to let go of our resentments, anger, and hatred. After sobriety, abandoning resentment just might be *the most important thing* we can do for ourselves and the people we love.

Notice that resentment is caused by real or *imagined* injury. That's an important point for us to remember, because chemically dependent people and codependents are experts at conjuring up wrongs we imagine have been committed against us. This exquisite sensitivity to injury cramps our lives and leads us to become guarded, suspicious, and jealous.

David's unreasonable resentments toward his wife and 25-year-old son very nearly cost him his home and family. A 55-year-old construction worker and alcoholic, Dave was arrested for drunk driving as he was heading home from an out-of-town job site. It was Saturday night, Dave was a stranger in town, and it was his *third* arrest for DWI. Bail was set at $10,000.

He used his one call to phone his wife, Doris. "Get me the hell out of this stinking jail," he ordered. "I don't care what it takes, but get me out!"

In a panic, Doris called their son, Steve. The two of them piled in the car and drove three hours to the town where Dave was.

"Sorry," the jailer politely informed them, "but we can't accept a check for bail. We need ten percent to let him out. That's a thousand dollars. In cash."

"But it's Saturday night!" Steve protested. "Where can we get that much money? Our check is good. Look, I've got a check guarantee card."

The officer was unimpressed. "Try a bail bondsman," he suggested. "But they won't take checks either."

Summoning every ounce of courage, Doris called a district court judge at home at 2:00 A.M. to ask for a reduction in bail. "No!" the judge thundered, "and if you want to talk to me again call my office at nine o'clock on Monday." He slammed down the receiver with a resounding crash.

"Please," Steve pleaded with the jailer. "At least let us see him so he'll know we're trying."

"Visiting hours are Tuesday and Thursday," the jailer informed him.

"But . . . ."

"No." One look at the jailer's face told Steve it was no use arguing.

On Monday afternoon, Dave appeared in court for arraignment. Remembering the small fines levied against him for his other two DWI convictions, he decided to plead guilty and get the whole mess over with.

"Ninety days in the county jail," the judge declared, "and a fine of one thousand dollars."

Stunned, Dave was led away to begin his sentence.

On Tuesday, Doris sat opposite Dave, a glass partition between them, tears streaming down her face.

"You bitch!" Dave hissed. "This is your fault. Why didn't you get me out of here? You and that no-good son of yours."

"We tried," she said. "But —"

"Don't give me that crap. If you'd gotten me out of here, I wouldn't have pleaded guilty. I could have gotten a smart lawyer. It's your fault I'm in here. You and that judge. You probably cooked this up together to make me stop drinking."

"That's not a bad idea," Doris conceded. "I wish I'd thought of it."

"See! You've as much as admitted it! You left me here to rot while — "

"Steve and I tried to get you out," she explained, "but we didn't have enough money."

"Like hell!"

"They wanted cash."

"You should have gotten it somehow. You could have put up the house for collateral, you could have — "

"It was Saturday night!"

"That doesn't matter. I counted on you to get me out of here and you betrayed me." He clenched his fists. "It's a good thing this sheet of glass is between us or I'd . . . ."

Dave sincerely believed his wife and son were to blame for his predicament! He imagined they had betrayed him. The fact that *he* had made the decision to plead guilty meant nothing to him. All that counted was that he had told Doris to get him out of jail and she had failed.

Dave was crippled by resentment, made angry by an imagined betrayal. A fancied wrong turned him hateful. He resented unreasonably, blaming his wife and son for his own mistakes. Unreasonable resentment poisons our lives.

Eventually Dave got sober in A.A., but he refused to let go of this resentment until, no longer able to take his accusations and ill will, Doris filed for divorce.

The shock of divorce papers woke Dave up. Fearing the loss of his wife of 35 years, he agreed to seek counseling from a therapist who understood both alcoholism and unreasonable resentment. The counselor told Dave and Doris that if they wanted to fully recover and if they wanted to save their marriage they would have to *straighten out their thinking*.

Resentment always has at its base certain negative, irrational thoughts. We need to figure out *which* irrational thoughts are making us so angry.

For Dave, it was the irrational idea that his wife and son *should* have somehow managed to rescue him from a problem over which they had no control. He futher believed that, regardless of the obstacles, they could have gotten him out *if they really wanted to*. He concluded, wrongly, that he had spent 90 days in jail because his wife and son didn't care enough to help him. He ran these thoughts over and over in his mind, until he made himself miserable and unbearable to live with.

Now, STOP: Think for a minute. Are you carrying around an unreasonable resentment? Do you run negative, blaming statements through your mind until you're so upset you can hardly sleep? If you're truly honest, you probably have at least one resentment that's causing you trouble. Stop right now, get a piece of paper and pencil, and write your resentment(s) down. Write down the name of the person you resent, then in one sentence, write down why you are resentful.

Your resentment list might look something like this:

I'm resentful at . . .	*Because . . .*
My mother	She tries to run my life. She refused to loan me five hundred dollars when I asked even though she had it. She gossips about me to her friends.
My neighbor	He reported me to the Child Protective Agency because I slapped my son.
My husband's ex-wife	She got a huge property settlement. She doesn't have to work and I do.
My husband	He forgot our anniversary.

This is an important exercise because, while it's easy for us to sit back and say, "Boy, that Dave, does he ever have a case of stinking thinking," it's extremely difficult for us to see our own totally unreasonable beliefs and thoughts. We can't rid ourselves of our resentments until we *recognize* them. Save your resentment list, because we're going to come back to it.

Psychologist Raymond Novaco tells us that anger and resentments are incited, maintained, and inflamed by "self-talk," the things we say and think to ourselves. We dwell on injustices and resentments, letting them smolder on for hours, days, weeks, months, even years after the initial provocation has passed. We may live in the present, but our emotions are stuck in the superglue of the past. We often don't recognize our own stinking thinking.

The key to becoming unstuck, to getting control of our anger, is changing our negative self-talk to positive self-talk. This is called cognitive or rational theory. Basically, cognitive theory tells us that our negative emotions have at their base uncertain negative, irrational thoughts. Negative feelings are caused by negative thoughts. To change the way we feel, we must change the way we think.

This is *very* important for us to understand. If we can't accept the simple fact that our thinking controls our feelings, we'll never be able to change, we'll never be able to find the key to happiness. Our lives will continue to be filled with conflict, tension, and resentments.

Those of us who suffer from chemical dependency and codependency have another major problem that doesn't always look like it's related to anger, but it is. It's called *self-pity.* Self-pity is caused by negative self-talk.

We feel so sorry for ourselves because our family, friends, coworkers, lovers, the whole darn world doesn't give us what we want, need, and feel we deserve. As we're wallowing around in the pity pot, we seldom stop to consider whether what we want from our family and friends is *reasonable.* Like Dave, we make an unreasonable demand and are devastated when it isn't met. To complicate things, some of our demands are never voiced. We just expect other people to *know* what we want.

How unreasonable can you get? Self-pity is anger, plain and simple. We're angry that life isn't fair, that it's full of hardship and disappointment. We think of ourselves as victims tossed around by an uncaring world. We're strong believers in luck. Bad luck for us; good luck for everyone else. And we're blamers. Who do we blame? Anyone who's handy: spouse, kids, Exxon, the Commies, the Tralfamadorians . . . .

Both Dave and Doris suffered from intense self-pity; Dave because he felt his wife and son had betrayed him and Doris because she was unjustly being blamed for something she had no control over. Psychologist Gary Emery says the most common targets of our blame are people we are dependent on. We say, "It was my husband's (or wife's, or parent's, or child's) fault."

We think thoughts like these:

I wouldn't be so tired all the time if my husband made enough money so I didn't have to work.

I wouldn't be stuck in a job I hated if my parents had encouraged me to get a better education.

I'd be more respected by my friends and have a better social life if my wife weren't fat and if she had a better personality.

I wouldn't have had to spend ninety days in jail for my third drunk driving conviction if my wife had come up with a thousand bucks bail on Saturday night.

We're experts at this blame game. If we can't find a person to blame, we'll even blame God. Self-pity, resentment, and fault-finding are symptoms of the family disease of alcoholism. Part of our recovery process is fearlessly confronting these defects in our thinking.

Wait a minute! Hold it right there! Did I just hear you say, "Poor me, why is this all so hard? Why am I saddled with all these special problems?" Everyone has problems, so stop thinking of yourself as specially burdened.

Consider the things that make you angry. Your sloppy stepchild, your lazy colleague, your insensitive spouse, the car that won't start, the insolent salesclerk, the boss who refuses to recognize your worth, your mother-in-law with her critical smirk. The list is endless. We get lied to, manipulated, fooled. We get insulted, ridiculed, used. Life treats us unfairly, dammit! Doesn't that give us the right to be angry?

Listen. Every single person in the world has similar (or worse) troubles to face every day. We are part of a huge mass of humanity facing the difficult problems of everyday life. Our problems are no more burdensome than our next-door neighbor's. People who look like they are sitting on top of the world have just as many problems and tragedies as we do. They just handle them better! (Or seem to. Appearances can be deceptive!)

We are not special, but we can *become* special. We do that by learning to cope with our problems and angry feelings without destroying our self-esteem or trampling all over somebody else's feelings. We cope with our problems by learning to be accountable for our own happiness.

But, you say, your life has been nothing but one bad break after another. Your blood boils at the mere thought of the hassles family, bosses, and so-called friends have put you through! They *make* you angry and unhappy.

Not so. We make ourselves angry by some line of illogical thinking. We blame other people for our own troubles. We "catastrophize," we make mountains out of molehills, we turn everyday irritations into major calamities. We get angry because we're thinking (partly unconsciously), "It's not *right* that Doris didn't get me out of jail."

Or: "It will be *unbearable* if Mary is late with the Bergstrom report. I'll look like a jerk if she doesn't do her job right."

Or: "I'll just *die* if George forgets our anniversary!"

Or: "It's not *fair* that I'm stuck with this crummy job and Joe got a promotion."

Stop and think for a minute. Analyze your thinking. Listen to what you're saying to yourself, the self-talk that's going on when tense situations come up. We do have these kinds of thoughts and they indeed make us angry. Our *feelings* of anger are triggered by our negative, irrational, catastrophic *thoughts*. This is the main reason we sometimes get into such a state over minor annoyances. And here's a fact of life we had better not ignore. Chemically dependent people and codependents can't afford to get into a state over minor annoyances. We can't waste our energy turning molehills into mountains. We don't have time to spin our wheels catastrophizing some little do-dah into a major crisis.

Why not? Because we have *real* catastrophes to deal with. You know, like a swollen and bloated liver, damaged children, making amends to people we have hurt with our arrogant and selfish behavior, rebuilding a career left in the ashes of alcoholism or other drug dependency, rebuilding our lives.

We have *work* to do! If we are to fully recover, we must learn to put the petty irritations of everyday life into proper perspective. We must take responsibility for our own behavior and stop blaming other people for our mistakes.

So what if Roy B. hogged the floor at the last A.A. meeting and you didn't get to have your say? So what if Delbert was twenty minutes late coming home for dinner and the salad got soggy? So what if somebody stole your parking spot? So what if you got yourself in a jam and your wife (husband, parent, friend, child) couldn't or didn't rescue you?

For this, you're ready to start World War III? For this, you'll develop a resentment? You'll risk your recovery by stubbornly clinging to that resentment? Life is too short, recovery too precious to squander our serenity on petty grievances.

We can learn how to cope with our unreasonable resentments. First, we must forcefully analyze away the illogical and self-defeating commentary that's running through our minds. Second, we must practice (and practice and practice) using positive, rational, logical self-talk.

For example, ask yourself, "Will I *really* die if George forgets our anniversary? Is it really so *awful* if I have to remind him? Is it a *crime* for him to be absentminded? So what if I have to drop a few hints for him to get the message? In most ways, he really does *try* to be a good husband. I wish I didn't have to remind him of important things, but it really is just a teensy little flaw in his character compared to his good points."

The conclusion is, you won't die, and it isn't necessary to create a torrent of unpleasant emotions over George's oversight. He probably feels bad enough. And if he still doesn't remember after you remind him, well, you'd better talk about what's really going on, instead of jumping to conclusions. Practicing this kind of rethinking — positive, rather than negative self-talk — we can rid ourselves of old resentments and prevent new ones from forming.

Let's take a look at some of the irrational thoughts that make us angry and resentful. Answer true or false.

1. I have often been treated unfairly.
2. I wouldn't have so many problems if other people treated me better.
3. I can't stand it if someone lies to me.
4. It really upsets me if someone snubs me.
5. If someone behaves badly, they should be punished.
6. It really ticks me off if things don't go the way I planned.
7. What happens to me usually depends on luck.
8. I've had so many unfair things happen to me in my lifetime that I'll never get over them.
9. There is no good excuse for breaking a promise.
10. If I have to *ask* my wife (husband, child, friend, lover) for a favor, it's not really worth having.
11. If someone really cares about me, they'll know how I feel about certain things without having to be told.
12. If someone hurts me in some way, I have the right to get even with them.

Answering true to even one or two of these questions suggests that you have a habit of blaming, resenting, or catastrophizing because of irrational thinking patterns. These kinds of thoughts are highly illogical and unfounded because they're based on the idea that we have the God-like ability to judge how other people should and should not be allowed to behave. Plus, we expect other people to be able to read our minds and behave accordingly. When they don't, boy, do we ever get angry! Angry and resentful.

CHAPTER SEVEN
Conquering Our Common Conceits

In Chapter Six we saw how our irrational thinking and negative self-talk fill us with resentment, an especially dangerous resentment that thwarts, undermines, and sabotages recovery. Recovery can also be hindered by Common Conceits generated by the strange notion that the world — and the people in it — should perform just so, to meet our expectations and our needs.

The Big Book of Alcoholics Anonymous[1] aptly describes the alcoholic as an actor who wants to run the whole show. He not only wants to be the star, he wants to be the director. This characterization applies to a broad spectrum of chemically dependent people.

If only we could get people to behave — to act the way we want them to. When the show doesn't come off just exactly right (it *never* does), we become angry, indignant, and self-pitying. We grit our teeth and fume. The muscles in our jaws tighten like clamps. Frustrated and angry, we hold others responsible for botched and bungled performances. Nitwits! Idiots!

If it weren't for the inept bunglers, we could be happy. If they'd just listen and pay attention to us and do what we *want* them to do. If they'd only act *right*, for heaven's sake. But they don't and they won't!

To expect others to meet our expectations is a prime Conceit. It's time to deflate it, and at the same time, let some air out of other cherished illusions and Common Conceits.

COMMON CONCEITS
I'm right, and you're wrong.
I'm right, and they're wrong.
I'm right, and the whole dang world is wrong.

---

[1]The Big Book is *Alcoholics Anonymous,* published by A.A. World Services, New York, N.Y. Available through Hazelden Educational Materials.

Alcoholics, other chemically dependent people, and codependents suffer from these conceits on a grand scale. Dr. Bob and Bill W. recognized this years ago. They understood completely the role delusions, anger, perfectionism, grandiosity, self-pity, and irrational thinking play in keeping alcoholics from full recovery.

But how do we go about deflating the Common Conceits? A.A.'s Fourth Step is a wonderful example of how we can straighten out our thinking by doing a fearless and searching moral inventory. Taking an honest inventory can, indeed, puncture some of our conceits.

But taking an honest inventory is not as easy as it sounds. To better recognize and grapple with the Common Conceits, it helps to understand what we call "The Wanting Sickness."

The Wanting Sickness

Much of our anger and emotional confusion can be traced to the *Wanting Sickness*. We *want* certain things so badly, we can make ourselves physically and emotionally sick when we don't get them. Some of our wants are concrete, tangible things that, with a little effort, can be within our reach:

I want a chocolate ice cream cone.
I want a new pair of shoes.
I want to go to the beach.

Our most basic wants are intangible and abstract. Almost all humans have these wants even if we don't admit it out loud:

I want love, approval, recognition.
I want to be attractive, accomplished, admired.
I want to be happy.

These wants are absolutely normal. There's nothing wrong with wanting ice cream, new shoes, or love. But we get in trouble with our wants when we begin to expect other people to fulfill our wishes for us or when our wants are irrational and unreasonable. These are the Conceits, the wants, that inevitably lead to anger. For example:

I want *you* to behave perfectly and to meet my needs.
I want *you* to make me feel happy and secure.
I want *you* to love me no matter how I treat you.

Do you see the pattern here? We expect other people to follow a perfect code of conduct (of our design). We want them to be the source of our happiness and security. We want their love and approval regardless of how we may act. What happens when our expectations aren't met? We're devastated. "Not fair!" we cry. "Life isn't supposed to be like this!" With wonderfully warped logic, we accuse, "You're bad for disappointing me!" And for every disappointment we build a resentment. We're architects of venom and vengeance. Deep down, we grudgingly concede, *There must be a better way*.

Good news. There *is* a better way. We need to learn how to tell the difference between a reasonable want and an unreasonable demand. We need to identify and eliminate Common Conceits. Sound familiar? It should, because that's the message of the Serenity Prayer. If you don't already know it, make it your own right now, by taking a few minutes to memorize it.

The Serenity Prayer is an all-purpose, all-weather tool for tightening, straightening, and calibrating faulty and malfunctioning thought processes. The Serenity Prayer never wears out, and it's guaranteed to work — if used regularly as directed.

So memorize it and repeat the Serenity Prayer quietly to yourself whenever you start dwelling on the unfairness of life.

THE SERENITY PRAYER

God grant me the Serenity
to accept the things I cannot change,
Courage to change the things I can,
and Wisdom to know the difference.

Many of the things we want are totally unreasonable and outside of our control. We want what we can't have, but we lack the serenity to accept the limits of reality.

Examples:

I want my life to be uncomplicated. (Reality: Everyone's life is complicated. The world is complex; the universe is complex; even the social life of termites is extraordinarily complex.)

I want to be four inches taller. (Reality: I'm not going to grow any more.)

I want to be able to drink like a social drinker. (Reality: I'm an alcoholic and I can't handle booze.)

Other wants are attainable if we work for them, but we become angry when they don't come to us automatically. We lack the courage to change the things we can.

Examples:

I want lots of money, a nice house, and a fast car (but I don't want to find a job and work my way up from a minimum wage).

I want to be attractive (but it's too much trouble to fix my hair, coordinate my wardrobe, and exercise three times a week).

I want to save my marriage (but not if I have to change, go to counseling, and quit drinking).

Some of our wants are vicious:

I want to get even with you for hurting me.

I want to hurt you because you didn't do what I wanted.

I want to make trouble for you because I'm envious of what you have.

When we don't get what we want, our first thought is: "Whose fault is it?" We're imprinted with the idea that if something bad happens, *someone bad* must have caused it, and that bad person must be punished to set things right. We think we have the obligation to get even, to settle the score, to let *them* know they can't get away with treating us this way. Thus, our resentments are born, nurtured, and energized.

How we handle our resentment depends on our temperament and anger style. A Bulldozer might yell and threaten, a Soulful One might sulk and seek quiet revenge. Whatever our style, if our responses are based on irrational thinking and negative self-talk, we spread confusion and bitterness, not harmony and understanding.

So, you ask, what do we have to do to *change*?

Practice Makes Perfect

Self-help writers sometimes promise that becoming a healthy, happy, rational person is easy. They lie! They know we want a quick fix, a way to remake ourselves overnight, an *effortless* way to become happier, slimmer, more sociable, less shy, more assertive and successful. All dreams and illusions. An old saying goes, "There's nothing wrong with dreaming if you wake when the bell rings."

Listen: The bell's ringing *now*.

Changing our irrational thinking and negative self-talk — getting our anger under control — is hard work. *Commitment* and *practice* are the key words to improving ourselves — practice, practice, practice. Skimming through this book (or any other book) won't change our behavior. But we can change!

These are the things we need to practice in order to rid ourselves of the irrational thinking patterns that are interfering with our recovery process.

1. *Accept responsibility for our own behavior*. The "Big Book" says an alcoholic is an extreme example of self-will run riot. Because we always want to have our own way, we trample on the feelings of other people, then we're surprised when they retaliate. Although we blame them for hurting us, if we are really honest with ourselves, we can look back and see how our selfish decisions set us up to be hurt. We have to accept that our problems are basically of our own making. Accepting responsibility for our thoughts, feelings, and actions is the first step toward constructive improvement. When we don't accept the responsibility for our own shortcomings we become stuck; stuck in our anger, resentments, and unhappiness. A major obstacle to acceptance is lack of awareness. That leads us on to relapse.

2. *Become aware of our negative self-talk*. We're so used to blaming and catastrophizing we usually aren't aware of what we're thinking and telling ourselves. Listen to your thoughts. You're probably making yourself angry with a lot of "what if" statements. "What if this terrible thing happens?" or, "I couldn't stand it if . . . happens!" or, "She shouldn't have

61

done . . . !" or, "I'm going to kill him if I find out . . . !" or, "Only an inconsiderate boob would . . . !" or, "You should have known that . . . ."

A lot of our anger-producing statements start out with, "It's not fair that . . . ," or, "It's not right that . . . ." We seem to think we are the ultimate judges of what is fair and right, of how other people should behave. And when they don't meet our expectations? Grrrrrrrr!

STOP! Go back and look at your resentment list. How many of your resentments are caused by negative and irrational self-statements? For example . . .

My mother has no *right* to interfere in my life. She's a bitch for hassling me.

My neighbor *shouldn't* have turned me in for beating my son. He's bad for causing me trouble.

Go through your entire list and make a note of the self-statements you're using to keep each resentment alive.

This is an important exercise because it helps us become *aware* of our irrational and negative self-talk. A little introspection on our part will often turn up a ton of similar statements.

Now, let's continue our examination of the things we must do to rid ourselves of our unreasonable resentments.

3. *Become aware of the anger sequence.* Remember: Our negative thoughts control our negative feelings. The anger sequence goes something like this:

We think (and say) to ourselves, *I want something.* If we don't get it, we say, *I'm frustrated because I didn't get what I wanted.*

Our next thought is, *It's an awful and terrible thing that I didn't get what I wanted.*

Next, we lay blame by thinking, *Whose fault is it?* When we find a target for our blame, we think, *You shouldn't frustrate me. I deserve to get what I want.*

Then, we become judgmental. We say, *You're wrong and bad for frustrating me!*

Finally, the justification for our wrath: *You deserve to be punished because you're bad*!

Net result? A whole lot of resentment.

We usually aren't aware of these kinds of thoughts when they're flashing through our minds. But if we sit down and think about it for a while, we can see this is *exactly* what happens when we get upset about something. Maybe we don't use those precise words, but we follow the same process.

But we don't have to. We can . . .

4. *Take action to derail the anger sequence.* With rational thinking and positive self-talk, we can derail the anger sequence before it derails us. We can stop resentment cold in its tracks.

Denial

It all sounds pretty easy, doesn't it? Well, it's not really as simple as it looks because our emotions are complex. We have all built up defenses to protect our egos from pain. This is normal.

But chemically dependent people and codependents have another obstacle to face. It's called *denial*. We refuse to believe or admit we have a problem even when our lives may be falling down around us. Denial is a hallmark of alcoholism and the family disease of alcoholism. It's what prevents us from seeking treatment when we need it because we don't think there's anything wrong with us.

There's our Common Conceit rearing its head again! *It's their fault,* we say, *I'm the one who's been wronged.*

To rid ourselves of resentments we must confront our denial. But denial is a powerful thing. We can admit we are powerless over alcohol, seek help, become sober, *and still be in denial.* Oh, yes, we've admitted our problems with alcohol and other drugs, but what about the other areas of our lives? Does sobriety turn us into perfect beings, halos gleaming, with no further personality defects? Of course not. For us, denial is as natural as breathing. But we *can* overcome it!

Defiance

One of the major components of denial is *defiance* which is defined as the will to oppose or resist, the contemptuous disregard of authority. What it means in practical terms is that we hate being told what to do. *We* want to run the whole show. Defiance probably stems from what the "Big Book" calls our need to be in control, to be right all the time.

Because we are naturally rebellious against authority, we have the tendency to keep ourselves sick, to really hurt ourselves, just to show the world nobody can push us around. And, to us, authority figures can be just about anyone. A few naturals for this role would be our parents, the boss, the police, and, of course, our spouses.

But what about the doctor who tells us we have to quit drinking or our liver will fall out? "Sure, Doc," we say. Then later, at the bar with our buddies, we laugh and ask, "Did you ever notice there are a lot more old drunks than there are old doctors?" Ha, ha.

Suppose we do sober up and the same doctor tells us we have the beginnings of emphysema and we must quit smoking immediately. Do we? Or do we decide, as we light up outside his office, that we will be the judge of whether cigarettes are hurting us (cough), and no old quack's going to tell us how to run our lives?

That's defiance for you. We'll kill ourselves with our bad habits before we'll let somebody else tell us how to run our lives. We'll defy just about anyone — a counselor, a minister, our kids — who tries to help us, anyone who tries to tell us what to do, even when we *know* what they are saying is true!

Of course, depending on our temperament type, we display our defiance in different ways. A Bulldozer might yell, a Lightheart might make a few sarcastic cracks and walk away. Bricks and Soulful Ones, with their quiet wills of iron, may appear on the surface to be agreeable and cooperative. Their defiance is disguised. It comes out in the form of forgetfulness, lateness, incompetence, illness, or subtle sabotage.

The point is, because of our tendency toward denial, we don't always recognize our defiance and irrational thinking. We continue the blame game! *I'm right*, we say, *and they are wrong*.

STOP: Let's take another look at our resentment list, this time with an eye open not only to our unreasonableness and negativity, but also to denial and defiance. We're also going to start challenging our common conceits.

Your resentment list might look something like this:

I'm Resentful at . . .   *Because . . .*
My mother   She tries to run my life.
                              She refused to loan me $500.
                              She gossips about me.

Thoughts About Mother:
My Mother has no right to interfere in my life. (Defiance)
    Challenge: She's only trying to help me. Is it so awful for my mother to worry about me? Don't I turn to her for help? Why, then, should I resent it when she tries to help in a way that's different than I wanted? Do I feel defensive and guilty because I know I've behaved badly and have to ask her for help?

She's a bitch! (Insulting, blaming)
    Challenge: She's not so bad, a little irritable, but no more than I am. I've given her a lot of trouble and she's always stood by me. Is it a crime for her to complain once in a while? Am I being selfish? Am I resentful because she doesn't always do exactly what I want her to? Do I always do exactly what she wants me to? Are you kidding?

She should have given me the money. (Demanding)
    Why? Haven't I borrowed money from her before and not paid it back? Why should she have to cancel her vacation in order to pay my debts? I'm always saying I want to be independent, so is it really so terrible that she won't let me be dependent on her for money? Am I resentful because I want my mother to still take care of me like she did when I was a child? Isn't that unreasonable?

How dare she talk to her friends about me! (Self-righteous)
    Don't I talk to my friends about her? Haven't I criticized her endlessly to my friends and my sister? What am I afraid of? Do I fear she'll reveal some of the bad things I've done? Is it so

terrible for her to confide in her friends? Don't I do the same thing?

Use this process to challenge each of your resentments. Fearlessly attack all of your defiant, blaming, demanding, negative, denying, self-righteous thoughts and substitute rational and positive thoughts in their place. Then practice, practice, practice!

An important note: At first this process seems cumbersome, but with practice you can learn to use these techniques automatically, without resorting to pencil and paper. But for now, while you are learning, it's important to set your thoughts on paper where you can see them clearly.

And keep in mind this is not a one-shot deal! Many of our resentments are so deeply embedded that we must challenge and rechallenge them over a period of days and weeks before we can *really* let that resentment go.

Don't forget to use this process for *new* resentments, too. It's easier to prevent a bad feeling if we face it directly, right now, when it first starts to bug us.

Okay, you've got your resentment list and you're ready to go, ready to clean house and get rid of all your old angry, hateful feelings with fresh, new, positive, rational thinking. But what about those situations where your anger isn't caused by a *fancied* wrong or injury? What if you're being rational and positive all over the place, but the other guy is really honestly and truly doing you wrong? What do you do when you need to express your anger and confront someone who is treating you badly?

Well, there's a right way and a wrong way to do everything, and the wrong way is to try to get everybody else to do it the right way. Let's take a look at some of the wrong ways for a minute. But first, let's take a Serenity Prayer break (fill in the blanks).

God grant me the Serenity
to _____ ,
_____ to change the things I can,
and _____ to know the difference.

66

CHAPTER EIGHT

The Ventilation Trap

"You go to hell!" Janet screamed into the telephone. She slammed down the receiver and said, "That makes me feel better!"

"It does?" I asked, baffled. She'd just told off her boss and seemed proud of it.

"My shrink told me it's unhealthy to hold in my anger," she explained, her voice trembling slightly. "I have to unload my anger, I have to let it out, or . . . or . . . ."

"Or what?"

"Well, you know, it's bad to go around with your feelings all bottled up. Especially anger. It can really be dangerous to hold angry feelings in. Anger just builds up and turns inward and causes all sorts of terrible problems like depression and guilt and anxiety. Even ulcers and headaches. When I get angry I'm supposed to get it *out*, not let it stay inside me festering like an abscess. I'm supposed to express my feelings."

"What about your boss?" I asked. "What's she supposed to do with her anger?"

Janet seemed baffled for a moment, then hesitantly replied, "Let it out, of course."

"I don't think I'd like to work in a place where my co-workers yelled at me whenever I did something they didn't like," I said. "In fact, I'd hate it!"

Janet shrugged. "That's your hang-up. I believe in letting people know how I feel. If they can't handle it, that's their problem." A week later, Janet told me she'd lost her job. Seems she'd built up a reputation as a troublemaker. People didn't want to work with her. Is it any wonder?

The freewheeling, no-holds-barred blowup can cause us more problems than it cures. Contrary to popular belief, there's not an iota of evidence that taking the shackles off imprisoned rage will prevent depression, ulcers, guilt, or anxiety. Getting mad and yelling, shouting, telling someone off, hitting, or breaking things may make us feel better momentarily, but more often than not these outbursts make us feel worse — much worse, in the long run.

Why do we feel *worse*? When we get angry, certain physical changes take place in the body. The pulse quickens and blood pressure shoots up. Breathing speeds up. The muscles contract and tense up. The digestive system changes. Adrenalin (the fight or flight hormone) is released. Blood sugar levels go up, then down.

These are just some of the physical changes that take place in our bodies when we get mad. True, these physical responses *can* give us chronic high blood pressure or problems with our stomach and bowels or tension headaches. But spontaneously releasing rage isn't the cure. Recent research clearly shows that expressing anger while we're upset does not defuse our anger, does not make the whirlpool of emotions subside. Instead, it nearly always makes the physical responses of the body — and our anger — more intense.

An uninhibited outburst of anger carries an additional hazard. It encourages the target of our anger to retaliate against us. As a tool for anger management, ventilating our feelings simply does not work. Unless, of course, our goal is to intimidate the people around us, to browbeat them into submission with the fierceness of our temper. If that's the case, we still have a *long* way to go in our recovery process.

The point is that while ranting and raving or beating each other with foam bats may be chic and expressive, it's also childish and ineffective. Worse, it can be downright counterproductive.

And remember, for us, the wholesale expression of anger is all tied up with feelings of fear and guilt. Trying to untangle and separate these interwoven emotions can be a painstaking task. So forget everything you've heard about the importance of letting it all hang out. It doesn't work.

Three Myths

MYTH #1:   THE BEST WAY TO DEAL WITH AN-
GER IS TO EXPRESS IT OPENLY AND
FORCEFULLY.

MYTH #2:   VENTILATING ANGER MAKES US
FEEL BETTER.

MYTH #3:   TELLING PEOPLE OFF IS A GOOD
WAY TO AVOID ULCERS (OR WORSE
AILMENTS).

If ventilating anger doesn't work, then what does? Certainly not ignoring it, or suppressing it and hoping it will go away. No. What we have to do is follow several steps. First, we must acknowledge our feelings to ourselves. Second, we must identify what thought or situation is triggering those feelings. Third, we must assess what changes, if any, we can make in the triggering thought or situation. Then we take action.

One of the actions we may choose to take is to express our indignant feelings by confronting the target of our anger. Sometimes that is the proper and healthy course to take. But before we puff up with righteous indignation and lambast our foe, we need to closely examine our own feelings and motivation.

This is especially important if we are already chronic complainers, always crabbing about how terrible life is and how disappointed and ticked off we are. This negativity becomes so habitual and ingrained that we don't even notice how frequently sour mutterings drift from our lips.

The world-weary Woeful Ones suffer from a free-floating hostility about life in general and have an attitude that says, "I'm mad at the world." This attitude is caused by the mistaken belief that *we and we alone* ended up with the short end of the stick.

Forever Angry

Would you agree that chemically dependent people and codependents are nearly obsessed with how unfairly life has treated them? We've already talked about how we practically worship the idea that we *deserve* to have what we want, but luck or fate or *they* prevent us from getting it.

Sandra is a good example of someone who is chronically mad at the world for treating her unfairly. You see, she *expected* her life to be so much *more* than it is.

The first thing she's mad about is her looks. At age 25 she's attractive enough to turn a few heads on the street, but she's short and a few pounds overweight and she has thin brown hair that frizzes in the rain. She hates her looks! She wants to look like Princess Diana — tall and slender with a silky mane of *thick* blonde hair. People like Diana have *all* the luck!

The next outrage in her life is her job. As a cashier in a busy store she makes better than average money, but she feels the job is really beneath her. She *belongs* in management, she just knows it, but her boss won't even consider her for a promotion because she dropped her business classes at the community college.

"Why do I need to know all that garbage anyway?" she complains, a note of petulance in her voice. "There ought to be an easier way to get a good job besides having to go to boring school and working like a dog for ten years before anyone recognizes how much you're worth!" She wishes she had more money; that would make her happy.

Then, there's her father. *He* has money, but refuses to buy her a new car even though he knows she needs one desperately. She has to drive around in an old clunker that's five years old. It's positively embarrassing! If she only had parents like her girlfriend Brenda's, life would be a whole lot easier.

And her boyfriend Bob! He actually expects her to contribute part of her salary for the down payment on the house they want to buy after they get married. If she looked like Princess Di, a man with enough money to support her would have fallen in love with her. Then, if she wanted to work, she could spend her money on clothes and vacations and fun things instead of having to support herself. Why did life have to be so hard and complicated and unfair? It just wasn't right!

How does Sandra cope with the hardships in her life? She drinks. And takes pills. She blames her father, a recovering alcoholic, for many of her problems. And when he tries to talk to her about her abuse of chemicals, she scoffs at him. "You're one to talk," she accuses. "I'm nowhere near as bad as you were. Just because *you* don't drink anymore, you don't think anyone should. Well, I'll tell you something, Dad . . . if I'd had a normal childhood, I wouldn't be so unhappy now. So, don't lecture me about *my* drinking. I'm not *that* bad!"

Poor Sandra. Her negative thinking and unrealistic expectations make her feel deprived and angry and emotionally low. Denial, coupled with a refusal to take responsibility for her own feelings, also prevent her from taking a good look at her growing drinking and drug problem. She takes everyone's inventory but her own.

And she won't let go of her anger about the past — her father's alcoholism, her unhappy childhood, even the physical characteristics (shortness, curly hair, a predisposition to alcohol problems) she inherited from her parents. She's mad at the world because it hasn't given her the things she thinks other people (like Princess Di) get automatically. Her expectations are unreasonable. And she complains about it constantly.

She expects to get all the good things in life — love, money, a nice house and car, admiration, status, a good job — handed to her on a silver platter (perhaps with a bowl of cherries on the side). She thinks happiness and possessions come easily to other people. Little does she realize that for every man or woman who has been *given* what they want in life, there are a hundred thousand hardworking men and women who have had to *earn* their happiness and achievements.

Here's the tragedy: Sandra's behavior is common in members of alcoholic families. If she had started her own recovery process when she realized her father was an alcoholic, her outlook on life might be very different now. She could be happy. Instead, she's becoming dependent on drugs herself.

Are you like Sandra? Are unreasonable expectations and negative self-talk making you miserable? Ask yourself these questions:

1. Do you often feel that circumstances not of your making have deprived you of the good things in life?
2. Do you often feel your life would be a lot better if you had only married the right person?
3. Do you feel aggrieved because life seems so hard and complicated and unfair for you while other people have it easy?
4. Do you attribute much of your present unhappiness to the mistakes your parents made in raising you?
5. Do you believe a person's happiness and success in life depend a lot on luck, good breaks, and connections?

Answering yes to even one of these questions — and especially to all five — shows you may have unrealistic expectations about "the way it's supposed to be."

Remember, our anger starts with an *I want* self-statement. When we don't get what we want, we start asking, "Whose fault is it?" And we always find someone to blame. Our chronic hostility spills over into every aspect of our lives; we're primed to explode. If another car slips into the last parking space, if a salesclerk is rude, if your wife eats the last spoonful of peanut butter and *you* wanted that peanut butter on your toast. . . it's . . . it's *outrageous*, an affront, absolute proof that nothing ever goes your way! Every inconvenience, every disappointment becomes evidence of the unfairness of it all. And we let people know about it!

Of course, this attitude makes us a pain to be around. Our friends get fed up with our constant grousing and complaining and negativity. Pretty soon, they start to give us a little feedback, maybe some constructive criticism, perhaps a dose of our own medicine.

We grow defensive. We find fault with *them*. Ultimately, our friends find excuses to avoid us. And we can't understand why we always seem to get rejected. Quite simply, our hostility and negativity make us too difficult to be around. We've created what's called a *self-fulfilling prophecy*. We expect the worst, so we react with negativity and hostility. Because we act like such pills, other people don't want to be around us, thus confirming our belief that the world treats us badly. It's a vicious circle; a circle of our own making.

Acknowledging Our Hostility

Nearly a hundred years ago, William James, the father of American psychology wrote: "In rage, it is notorious how we 'work ourselves up' to a climax by repeated outbreaks of expression. Refuse to express a passion, and it dies. Count to ten before venting your anger, and its occasion seems ridiculous."

This is still good advice. Unfortunately, refusing to express an emotion is usually confused with pretending it's not there. That's not what we want to do. We don't want to become repressed and tightjawed, with brave little smiles pasted on our faces as we say, "One, two, three, nothing bothers me, four, five, six . . . ."

While instantaneously expressing our anger is not an effective way of coping with our feelings, *acknowledging* our emotions is an important first step. Somewhere down the line, we may choose to appropriately express our anger, but first we have a little homework to do.

It's important for us to recognize the difference between *expressing* and *acknowledging*.

Expressing means to reveal through speaking or behaving. To acknowledge something means to own it or admit it as true. We can acknowledge silently (to ourselves) or aloud to others. Does it seem like a small difference? It's not, and here's why.

A typical expression of anger might be something like, "Hey, you jerk! What the hell do you think you're doing? Are you stupid, or something? Either shape up or ship out! You hear me?"

This expression of anger is insulting, demanding, and accusing. It's also likely to provoke a retaliation: "Same to you, creep! Stick it where the sun don't shine!"

From there, the confrontation both escalates and deteriorates, with hurt feelings all around and very little solved. When we spontaneously express our feelings without taking time out to analyze the situation and to calm down a little, we run a big risk of saying things we don't mean, of blowing small irritations out of proportion, and feeling like an absolute idiot an hour or a day later.

When we acknowledge our feelings, we make a statement: *I feel angry . . . I feel hurt . . . I feel guilty.*

An *I feel* statement is neither accusing nor blaming. We are simply admitting we are experiencing a certain emotion. This is called an *I* statement, as opposed to a *You* statement. *You* statements almost always make other people defensive and less likely to cooperate with us. Notice the difference between saying *I feel angry* and *You make me angry.*

Learning to make *I* statements is the first small step in taking responsibility for ourselves. We're *owning* our feelings instead of *blaming* something or someone else.

So, when we feel the first prick of irritation — when our lips are trembling with the desire to blurt out, "Hey, jerk!" — we must stop ourselves and ask, "What am I feeling?" Our next question is, "Why am I feeling this way?" Once we discover what is triggering our anger, we need to ask, "What can I do about it?" The final question is, "What am I *going* to do about it?"

These four simple questions can help us change. We don't have to be complaining, unhappy, and chronically angry people if we use our powers of rational thinking to analyze our unrealistic expectations and negative self-talk. But remember, this process takes PRACTICE.

THE FOUR QUESTION CHALLENGE

When you feel yourself getting angry, STOP. Ask . . .

1. WHAT AM I FEELING?
2. WHY AM I FEELING THIS WAY?
3. WHAT CAN I DO ABOUT IT?
4. WHAT AM I *GOING* TO DO ABOUT IT?

The first question helps us acknowledge and own our feelings. This is an important step because it puts a momentary halt in the middle of the anger sequence. When we focus our attention on owning our feelings, we are prevented, at least for a minute or two, from laying blame on someone or something else.

The second question helps us identify what's triggering our emotion. It forces us to analyze the anger sequence and our own irrational thinking and self-talk.

The third question helps assess our options. Are there positive changes we can make to improve the situation? What are they? Are we fighting to change something over which we have no control? Are we angry because of our unreasonable expectations and irrational thinking?

The fourth question asks us to make a decision. We've analyzed our options, now which one(s) will benefit us the most without harming other people? Will we be accountable for our own feelings and actions or will we continue the blame game?

In our using days, we were enmeshed in confusion, pain, and discontent. In recovery, we have the opportunity to create harmony and healing. The choice is ours.

You see, as we ask ourselves that last question, "What am I going to do?" we are choosing whether we will sow discord or peace, whether we will cling to our resentments or abandon them, put them behind us as useless and destructive thoughts.

Again, we come back to an *I want* statement. If we choose *I want* to be right, *I want* you to do my bidding, *I want* to run the show, *I want* revenge, then our poor attitude continues.

If we choose *I want* to make amends, to live and let live, to accept my own shortcomings, and to take my own inventory, then we are on the road to recovery.

But even in recovery, *expect to continue having some anger and trouble nearly every day of your life.*

"What?" you ask. "You mean all this work and practice, and we're still going to have problems?"

Oh, yes, it's true. The magic of self-help has limits: People live happily ever after only in fairy tales and romance novels.

Trouble and strife and irritations will still come our way. Blue days will descend, resentments will boil, minor annoyances will drive us up the wall. We may even have a major disaster or two.

But we can guarantee this: By practicing the Four Question Challenge we are in a better position to roll with the punches. We can face life head-on and confident, because we're armed with serenity and courage and wisdom, ready to fearlessly challenge our conceits, negativity, denial, and defiance.

Are you ready for the next challenge? This is a biggie! It's time for the inevitable — *the confrontation*.

CHAPTER NINE

Wrangling Without Rancor

The "Big Book" advises us to avoid argument and retaliation, to shun rancorous wrangling for our sobriety's sake.

"An excellent suggestion," we say. "We agree wholeheartedly! But . . . ."

But what?

"But how do we deal with the arrogant egotists and addle-pated blockheads who seem to be lurking around every corner to subvert our serenity?"

There's the rub. We rid ourselves of disabling resentments. We try hard to overcome our denial. We practice positive self-talk and make efforts to overcome our Common Conceits. And we use the Four Question Challenge. We can see we've made progress. But . . . .

But what about those times when someone we are close to behaves in a way that is irritating, inconsiderate, disruptive, or even harmful to our recovery? Should we turn away, count to ten, and meditate on green thoughts in a green glade?

There are times when we simply *must* speak up firmly for our rights. If *we* don't speak up, nobody will. We have to let people know what's on our minds. We don't transmit thoughts on a special "spouse wavelength" and our spouse doesn't have a built-in receiver that picks up random ruminations of discontent.

Betty was furious. Her house smelled like a tavern and she blamed her husband, Calvin. His brother had come to visit for a few days and he packed the refrigerator with beer and used the coffee cups for ashtrays.

"I don't expect Cal's brother to quit drinking just because we did," Betty said. "I wouldn't have minded if he'd put a beer or two in the refrigerator. But he'd put two six-packs in. And smoke! My God, he was a chain smoker, and I don't even have any ashtrays. At least he could have gone out on the porch instead of smelling up the whole house."

"Did you say anything to Cal or to his brother?"

"Well, no," Betty said righteously. "If Cal really loved me, he'd know how I felt."

Not necessarily. Too often we try to send our thoughts and feelings out in a kind of code. We drop hints. We grimace or give pained looks. Or we engage in passive resistance. None of these ploys works. Worse, they can be *infuriating* to those we're trying to communicate with, because they're trying to understand us and we're doing charades.

Making *demands* doesn't work either because it's almost guaranteed to provoke resistance. Do *you* like to be ordered about? Well, neither does anyone else.

We need to be direct, but not dictatorial. We need to stop playing charades about our feelings, stop transmitting important thoughts to people who can't read minds. Our goal is to be assertive, to speak up firmly — but quietly — when the time is right.

Before we jump, of course, we must sort out whether the situation is one that *can* be improved through a gentle confrontation, or if it is something the other person simply can't do anything about. For instance, what good does it do to nag your wife if you don't like her ex-husband when he comes to visit the kids. What can *she* do about his irritating habits? There's no use getting all agitated and crabby and having big scenes about stuff that can't be changed. Fighting about things that can't be changed is wrong!

Preparing for the Confrontation

If we must confront — if a confrontation is needed to improve a bad situation — there *is* a way to go about doing it which promises at least a chance of a positive outcome, which means we make our point, maintain our self-respect, and don't totally demolish the other person. Our kind of confrontation is a well-thought-out, dispassionate, lovingly firm statement we make to a person we care about. During the confrontation, we point out how a certain behavior is causing trouble for them, or us, or other people. We explain how this can be changed, and, when possible, we make a commitment to do what we can to make that change easier.

Gather your facts and information and be ready to present *specific* examples of the behavior you are talking about. Also, have specific solutions to offer. (Of course, you've used your Four Question Challenge to analyze your resentment! Make sure your solutions are positive, reasonable, and attainable.)

Remember, this confrontation is meant to be a firm but loving statement. We don't want it to turn into a fight. It may take all our rational coping skills to prevent a battle, especially since we can expect a certain amount of resistance, denial, and defiance from the other people. After all, they're only human.

Rational Self-Talk Before the Confrontation

Psychologist Raymond Novaco suggests using the following kinds of self-statements to prepare for a confrontation:

- I can work out a plan for this situation.
- If I start getting upset, I know what to do.
- Time to relax. Take a few deep breaths. Be calm.
- This could be a touchy situation, but I can handle it.

The Confrontation

Pick a good time, when the other person is not distracted or involved in another activity; and pick a good place, where you can have privacy and no interruptions. But don't wait for the *perfect* time! The perfect time never comes.

Now, get serious. If you mean business, let your face show it. We can't expect the other person to take us seriously if we don't *act* serious.

Ted, who had been sober for six months, handled a serious problem with his wife this way. "Mary," he said one night after dinner. "I have something to tell you. Can we talk for a minute?"

Ted's face looked so grim, Mary immediately turned off the television and sat down on the couch. Ted sat opposite her and said, "I'm really bothered by the beer you've been keeping in the fridge for Ted Jr. and his friends."

"But," Mary objected, "they're over 21. Why shouldn't Teddy be able to have a beer when he comes for a visit? *He* doesn't have a drinking problem." Her voice fairly dripped with sarcasm.

Ted took a deep breath. *Stay calm,* he told himself. "No," he said agreeably. "Teddy doesn't have a drinking problem, but I do. I'm an alcoholic. I'm having a hard time facing that cold beer when I come home from work every night. I don't like having to struggle with temptation on a daily basis. I believe in 'out of sight, out of mind.' I feel like I'm being sabotaged in my efforts to stay sober."

"That's ridiculous," Mary replied indignantly. "You're being asinine!"

Pausing for a moment, Ted thought, *It's a shame Mary's acting the way she is, but I can handle it.*

Looking Mary straight in the face, he said, "I'm asking you for your help, Mary. I need your support. When you buy beer and bring it home, I begin to feel resentful. I'm afraid I'm losing confidence in your willingness to solve our problems together."

"You're the one with the problem!"

Ted swallowed hard and took another deep breath. *There's no need for me to get defensive*, he told himself. "Yes, Mary," he said. "I'm an alcoholic. I intend to continue attending my meetings and I intend to stay sober one day at a time. But I'm asking you to stop bringing beer home. It makes it more difficult for me to deal with my problem. But, you know, I thought we had agreed that this was a *family* problem. I wish you'd start coming to the meetings with me again."

Mary sighed, "Oh, I suppose so. If it will make you happy. We'll go tomorrow night. And I'll buy soda for Teddy. But you're the one with the problem, not me."

Ted smiled. *Poor Mary. She needs to save face by blaming me, but at least she agreed to go to the meeting. That's good.* He leaned forward and gave her a light kiss. "Thanks for agreeing to help me, sweetheart. I really appreciate it."

Did you notice how Ted handled the confrontation? He stayed calm, stayed on track, and used positive self-talk. He also quit while he was ahead, resisting the temptation to harangue his wife until she agreed with him in every detail. He let her save face as long as she agreed to his two major requests. We can learn from his example.

Confrontation Skills

- Pick a good time and place.
- Be serious and firm, but loving.
- State your concerns clearly and immediately.
- Use specific examples.
- Use *I* statements vs. *You* statements.
- Stay on track.
- Use rational self-talk to stay calm and reasonable.
- Present clear, reasonable, and positive solutions.
- State your commitment to solve the problem.
- Don't insist on 100% acquiescence to your every wish.
- Show your appreciation for cooperation.

The Fight

Whole books have been written extolling the beneficial aspects of fighting. Clears the air and all that. Relieves the tension, clears the complexion.

Not for us.

If we are wise, we will avoid fighting. Why? Because in our unguarded moments, it's easy for us to slip backward, away from recovery and towards unreasonableness and negativity. Fights usually accomplish nothing, unless we consider name-calling, accusations, fault-finding, hurt feelings, and splattered egos worthwhile endeavors.

Fighting builds resentments. We become so intent on being *right*, and proving our opponent wrong, that we say and do things we are later ashamed of.

Who needs it?

And listen: there's more than one way to fight. Bellowing and screaming is one way, the most recognized way. The silent treatment is another. And it's vicious. So, if we keep our mouths clamped tightly shut while we radiate hostility and slam doors, *we're fighting*. Silent fights can go on for days.

Can we avoid all fights?

Probably not. The most important thing we can do to avoid unnecessary fighting, is *watch out for pressure times*. The worst fights happen when we are tired and under stress.

RULE #1 FOR AVOIDING UGLY FIGHTS: WATCH OUT FOR PRESSURE TIMES, FATIGUE, AND STRESS.

When we're under stress, we start picking on each other, one thing leads to another, and whammo! We're fighting. It's not each other we're mad at initially, but when the tire goes flat on the way to the family reunion and we're already late, and the kids are fussing, and the spare tire is flat, too . . . .

Rational Self-Talk During a Fight

Dr. Novaco suggests these self-statements when we find ourselves losing our cool:

- I feel myself tensing up. Time to relax and slow down.
- Getting mad won't help this situation.
- It's reasonable to get angry, but let's keep the lid on.
- My anger is a sign. It's time to talk to myself.
- Just because I've already gotten angry doesn't mean I have to stay angry. I can calm down.

After the Fight

When the fight is over, when you've calmed down, *apologize*. Maybe you didn't start the fight, but did you do or say things to keep it going? Fearlessly examine your behavior, and make amends where necessary.

Calming Others

Pressure and tension are all around. Those close to us can succumb to the stress, turning themselves into time bombs, waiting for the slightest provocation to explode! If this isn't a *chronic* condition with our loved one, it can pay us to tiptoe around a bit until the crisis passes. Too often, when we see aggression, we match it. Boom! The fight starts.

One of the things we can do to head off a fight is to refuse to fight fire with fire. While the other person is coming apart, we *model calmness*.

How do we model calmness? Our face shows an unwrinkled forehead, eyes opened normally, nose not wrinkled, mouth not snarling. Our hands are open, not clenched, our movements slow and smooth, our voice gentle. This kind of demeanor is unthreatening, and not likely to provoke an outburst.

It also helps to *listen openly and sympathetically* to others, even if they aren't making much sense. At times, we all need to blow off steam. It's not necessary for us to challenge every word coming from their mouths.

If the other person does become too aggressive, it can help if we *reassure* them that less drastic alternatives exist and we are willing to help find those solutions. Reassurance can be offered with statements like, "It's all right, we've solved worse problems." "Don't worry. We can handle this one step at a time." "It'll be okay. We'll work it out."

One of the most important things we can do to calm another person is *help them save face*. Nobody wants to end up looking like a fool, and a person will often cling stubbornly to an idea they know is stupid rather than admit their mistake. We can ease the situation by not rubbing the other person's nose in his or her foolishness, by compromising, and by resisting the temptation to say, "I told you so."

Techniques for Calming Others

- model calmness
- listen openly and sympathetically
- reassure the other person
- help save face

Admitting Defeat

Linda did everything right and it almost drove her crazy. "I didn't know what was wrong with me," Linda admits. "I took my inventory, I worked on letting go of my resentments, I practiced rational thinking, I went into therapy. Still, my family life was miserable!"

Linda lived with her husband, Phil, and his fourteen-year-old daughter, Pam, from a previous marriage. Linda and Phil had been married for three years before Pam came to live with them. The girl's mother had given up on her.

"Pam was a handful," Linda says. "And Phil made it clear from the start that he wanted me to be Pam's friend, as well as her stepmother. It was a disaster from the start! Pam was surly and disobedient and into drugs. Phil refused to discipline her. I guess he suffered from the divorced father 'guilts.' Anyway," Linda continued, "the situation went from bad to worse. I work full time, but neither Phil nor Pam would help with the housework, which really infuriated me because before Pam came, Phil did share the chores. After a few months, I was exhausted."

Linda's counselor suggested Linda orchestrate a family conference, a structured confrontation where Linda could express her concerns clearly and ask Phil and Pam to take a fair share of the chores. The confrontation went off beautifully.

"Okay, okay, you're right," Phil agreed.

"Sure, sure, whatever you say," Pam sighed.

Nothing changed. More family conferences, more promises of cooperation. No follow-through.

"Phil and I were fighting all the time," Linda remembers. "Pam was totally out of control. And no matter what I did, nothing changed!"

Linda faced a heartbreaking reality: some people just won't change. They make promises, but they have no intention of changing and they don't care whether you like it or not.

If their annoying behavior is something minor, say, they *never* hang up their clothes or they put empty milk cartons back in the refrigerator, may we suggest you simply *lower your expectations*.

But what if it's something major? Like drug use or gambling or physical abuse. What then? Ann Landers, the advice columnist, poses this question to readers contemplating divorce: Decide if you'd be better off with or without the spouse. Then make your move.

If the problem is a big one, if it threatens your health, safety, or recovery, and if, after a loving confrontation, the other person is unwilling to start making some changes, you may not be able to continue the relationship, even if it is a family relationship.

The situation is heartbreaking and real. The decision is not one to be made in the heat of anger. Unfortunately, even our best efforts can't fix every relationship. We can only hope our coping skills can carry us through the painful transition in one piece.

The Limits of Reason

A story is told of a young man who believed he was dead. His psychiatrist finally hit upon a logical, rational way to convince the young man that he was very much alive. He taught the young man to tell himself over and over, "Dead men don't bleed, dead men don't bleed."

After the young man had practiced this bit of rational self-talk for a couple of weeks, the psychiatrist pulled out a pin and drew blood from the young man's finger. The young man gazed in astonishment and wonder as droplets of blood formed on his fingertip.

"Now what do you say?" the psychiatrist asked triumphantly.

"By God!" the young man exclaimed. "Dead men *do* bleed!"

The point of the story is, of course, that rational coping skills have their limits. We can be paragons of rationality and still come up against the unreasonable and illogical behavior of our friends, colleagues, and families.

We can't win 'em all.

CHAPTER TEN

Beyond the Serenity Prayer

Let's say we've made some clear progress: We've really begun to accept that there are some things we can't change. We've mustered up courage to begin changing some of the things we can. And we're slowly acquiring the wisdom to know the difference. But there's one more step, beyond the Serenity Prayer.

Forgiveness

To err is human, goes the old saying, and to forgive is divine. Unfortunately, too often we're inclined to carry our grudges openly and relentlessly. We keep our malice alive, giving lip service to forgiveness or leaving it to the divine.

Tennyson captured a common attitude toward forgiveness:

Forgive! How many will say "forgive," and find
A sort of absolution in the sound
To hate a little longer.

Then there are the implacable, unforgiving ones, like Hallie, so preoccupied with being wronged that forgiveness never comes to mind. Hallie hated her father. A reserved, no-nonsense type of man, Herb had never understood his eldest daughter's emotional intensity, her passion for living. And Hallie had never understood her father.

He had given her material things — fashionable clothes, a sports car. And he'd paid for her education. But he was a workaholic who spent little time with his family, and, except for material things, he'd ignored Hallie while she was growing up.

Seven years after she'd left home, Hallie was living in another state, but she still keenly felt resentment for the emotional neglect she'd suffered as a child.

Hallie felt constricted and inadequate, cheated and rejected, and it was her father's fault. Her therapist seemed to confirm Hallie's suspicions.

"How did you feel when your father ignored you?" the therapist asked.

"Confused," Hallie replied, "and depressed. I wanted him to show his love, I wanted his approval."

"You felt like he disapproved of you, then. It must have made you feel alone."

"Yes!" Tears brimmed in Hallie's eyes as she remembered the way her father used to shake his head and roll his eyes when she talked about her dreams and plans. "He never listened to me. And he always made me feel stupid!"

"Stupid?"

"Yes," Hallie said bitterly. "Stupid and weak and powerless. And I still feel that way."

"Give me an idea how it makes you feel now, how it affects your life."

"Oh, God, I'm so embarrassed," Hallie said. "Here I am, twenty-eight-years-old, and I still feel like a kid! I needed him to show me he understood and cared about me. But he didn't."

"It sort of sounds like you feel he really let you down, as though he cheated you."

"That's it exactly," Hallie confirmed. "I *was* cheated. And I want him to know it. I want to tell him. But I'm scared."

"It's really a scary thing to do, to let your father know your real feelings."

Through several more therapy sessions, Hallie came to believe that the only way she could rid herself of the demon of her hate and despair was to face her father, not as a child full of fear, but as an adult. She wouldn't let him intimidate her this time either. She wouldn't back down; she'd tell exactly how his coldness and neglect had hurt and damaged her.

And she had the perfect opportunity. Her father was retiring in a month due to his failing health and a big family party was planned. She could kill two birds with one stone by using her vacation time to visit her family and have it out with her dad.

The confrontation went according to plan. She blasted him with the facts, and when he tried to shut her up by changing the subject, she kept at him, throwing his faults in his face, documenting in painstaking detail the neglect she'd suffered, until he finally broke down. He cried.

For the first time in her life, Hallie saw her father show real emotion. She felt triumphant. Every last bit of her wrath had been vented, every resentment had been aired, her father — her big strong emotionless father — had finally been defeated.

Hallie's mother was furious. "How dare you speak to your father that way! After all he's done for you, and in his condition!"

"Don't worry, Mom," Hallie said confidently. "Now that everything's out in the open, we can deal with it honestly. We can have a real relationship as equals now." *And*, Hallie thought silently, *you're next on my list, Mom*.

The next day, Hallie flew back home feeling a sense of accomplishment and pride. The feeling was short-lived. Three weeks later her father was dead. His illness had been much more serious than Hallie had been willing to see.

Hallie was stunned. He had always seemed so powerful and indestructable. Her denial and resentment had blinded her. All the time to talk of the good things to come, the fantasy of a real relationship with her father, lay in ashes and dust.

And Hallie made an important discovery too late: She had loved her father — really loved him. But in her single-minded pursuit of revenge, she had neglected to let him know of her love and gratitude. She had turned bitter and selfish. Hallie's last memory of her father, and her father's last memory of her, was one of ugliness, recrimination, and persecution.

Two years later, Hallie is still struggling with her guilt and grief. She would do anything if she could turn back the clock to that fateful day and change history.

I asked Hallie, "If you had the chance to do it over again, with what you know now, what would you have said to your father?"

Hallie thought hard for a moment, then said, "I would go to him, put my arms around him, and say, 'I love you, Dad. I know you did the best by me that you could. Let's let bygones be bygones.' " Hallie sighed. "And if I still felt resentment? I'd go out to the highest hill and rail at the sky until I had no more strength left in me, then I'd drop to my knees and ask my Higher Power to give me the courage and wisdom to forgive my father for whatever he had done to hurt me. That's what I'd do if I had the chance."

Forgiving the Sins of Omission

Hallie's father had been guilty of what are called *sins of omission*. He had not beaten his daughter, or vilified her, or starved her, or thrown her out into the street. His mistakes were much less tangible — he had failed to understand Hallie's secret needs. He did what most good fathers of the 50s and early 60s did. He worked hard to provide his family with a nice home, good food, and a decent living. In those days, men didn't nurture; they provided. He did the best he could, but he made mistakes. *All parents make mistakes in raising their children.*

None of us is a perfect being; we will all make mistakes. Much of our anger is directed at people who weren't there when we needed them, people who disappointed us or let us down because they were so involved with their own concerns that *they failed to recognize what we needed from them.*

Listen: Sins of omission happen in every family, every marriage, every friendship. We cannot escape them! By forgiving those who have hurt us with sins of omission, we free ourselves from the burden of bitterness, hate, and isolation. While blame is one of the worst of human characteristics, forgiveness is one of the best. Forgiveness frees us to love again.

Self-Statements that Foster Forgiveness

- I know _____ did the best he or she could.
- Everyone makes mistakes. I know _____ _____ didn't mean to hurt me.
- That was then, and this is now. Let's start over from today.
- Grant me the strength to forgive _____ for what he or she did to harm me.
- I forgive _____ . My heart is filled with love.

Forgiving Sins of Commission

What about the person who has gone out of his or her way to harm us? A person who acted against us purposefully and with the full intent to cause us trouble? Or the one who just didn't care whether we were hurt or not? Do we forgive that person?

Yes, if the act of forgiveness will relieve us of the burden of hate which is poisoning our recovery. We don't have to like that person, the way they acted, or what they did to us. We don't have to let him or her back into our lives. The "Big Book" suggests we realize that perhaps the person who wronged us was sick, suffering from a spiritual illness. It suggests we show him or her the same pity we would show a sick person.

So, yes. It is wise to forgive, but we don't have to forget. By not forgetting what the person did, we can avoid trouble in the future. It is unwise to trust a person who has proven to be untrustworthy. Forgiving that person does *not* mean we have to trust him or her again. To do so would be foolish and stupid on our part. Alan had trusted his brother to invest a considerable sum of money in the stock market. Instead, the brother had used Alan's money at the race track and lost it all. Alan found the strength to forgive his brother, but he never again allowed his brother access to his money or business.

As a child, Christine had been sexually abused by her father. She forgave him, but spent very little time with him and refused to allow him to be alone with his grandchildren.

Bob quit drinking on his own, but he still remained ill-tempered, pessimistic, and argumentative. Every holiday season, he visited his parents and created chaos with his foul language and temper tantrums. His parents forgave him, but when he refused to seek treatment for his problems, they banned him from attending family gatherings until he agreed to make some positive changes.

> TO ERR IS HUMAN.
> TO FORGIVE, DIVINE.
> TO FORGET, FOOLHARDY.

Forgiving Ourselves

Oh, the unspeakable shame of our own sins! If we can forgive others, can we not forgive ourselves? Are we not deserving of the same tolerance that we show others?

Forgiveness is an act of healing. If we look beyond our guilt, recognize our wrongs, and work fearlessly to correct our mistakes, then we have the right to forgive ourselves for both our sins of omission and commission. If we are unable to forgive ourselves for the wrongs we have committed in the past, we may be condemning ourselves to a lifetime of fear and guilt. A.A.'s Fourth and Fifth Steps are excellent devices to help us come to terms with our past mistakes.

A WARNING:
FORGIVENESS DOES NOT GRANT US THE RIGHT TO CONTINUE OUR DESTRUCTIVE WAYS.

Forgiveness grants us the freedom to heal, to start afresh, to make amends, to love.

Forgiveness is not the end, it is the beginning.

SUGGESTED READINGS

ANGER

ANGER: The Misunderstood Emotion, by Carol Tavris, Simon and Schuster, 1982, 302 pp. with notes, bibliography, and index.

An up-to-date, readable book by a social psychologist who examines anger research and takes issues with traditional psychological dogma about anger. Explores the world of the anger industry, and explodes the value of ventilation — a widely prescribed exercise for dealing with angry feelings, which in fact may make them more intense and less manageable.

Anger and Aggression, by James R. Averill, Springer-Verlag, 1982, 390 pp., with notes, bibliography, and index.

For the reader who wants to take an in-depth look at anger and aggression. Heavy on research and theory, light on anger management techniques. An excellent reference book — will settle any controversial wrangling about the subject of anger.

STRESS MANAGEMENT

Progressive Relaxation, by Edmund Jacobson, M.D., University of Chicago Press, 1929. (There are other, less expensive, recent editions of this book available in paperback.)

This is a classic — as valid now as it was when it was first published. Jacobson, a physician, gives a detailed explanation of tension and explains the value of learning how to relax. His "progressive relaxation" exercises have been used, adapted, and recommended by many prominent psychologists and psychiatrists. Jacobson was the first to experimentally demonstrate what has become the fundamental rationale for relaxation: "On rational grounds no less than on the basis of current physiological knowledge, it seems permissable to say that *to be excited and to be fully relaxed are physiological opposites.* The rule or law thus stated would seem to apply to many conditions familiar in medical practice and would suggest that the role of applied relaxation might be directly efficient."

Jacobson's book *You Must Relax* (1962) presents an update of his original book on Progressive Relaxation, written for a more general audience.

The Relaxation Response, by Herbert Benson and Miriam Z. Klipper, Avon Books, 1976.

If you've tried Progressive Relaxation and found it takes too long, or that it's too complicated, then *The Relaxation Response* might be the quick fix you're looking for. Benson developed a twenty-minute relaxation exercise based on four basic elements: a quiet comfortable environment, a "mental device" (a single syllable repeated silently or in a soft, gentle tone), a passive attitude, and a comfortable position. His research shows that the Relaxation Response can be readily evoked by anyone using this "simple, mental, noncultic procedure" developed in Benson's laboratory. And it also shows that Relaxation Response creates a calm meditative state that is similar to that found in subjects who practice transcendental meditation.

Relax, edited by John White and James Fadiman, The Confucian Press, 1976.

Relax gives a potpourri of relaxation techniques and kindred methods for dealing with tension and reducing stress, including meditation, massage, self-hypnosis, biofeedback, and yoga. Includes selections from Benson's *Relaxation Response* and Jacobson's *Progressive Relaxation*, as well as readings from the works of Hans Selye, Aaron T. Beck, and others who have stressed the importance of relaxation and tension reduction in therapy.

This is a relatively inexpensive paperback and gives an excellent introduction to the whole area of stress reduction and relaxation. Includes a very useful bibliography.

NUTRITION

Alcoholism: The Nutritional Approach, by Dr. Roger J. Williams, University of Texas Press, 1959.

Dr. Roger J. Williams is a biochemist who pioneered research into the relationships between alcoholism and nutrition. Williams considers alcoholism to be a metabolic disease that can be prevented by sound nutritional practices, and he argues for the importance of nutritional factors in treatment.

The Recovery Handbook, by Gayle Rosellini and Mark Worden, DIN Publications, Phoenix, 1980.

Aimed at people recovering from chemical dependency, this was the first book to bring together concepts of nutrition, stress management, and cognitive coping responses (including rational thinking) in a self-help format. The subtitle — "What do you do after you say: 'I quit' " — hints at the basic theme. It's fairly easy to quit alcohol and drugs, but the real challenge is to stay clean and drug-free, and to avoid relapse. There are many ways to get sober, and many ways to stay sober, says *The Recovery Handbook*. And it offers insight into common nutritional practices that sabotage recovery and suggests specific easy-to-follow techniques for enhancing recovery.

COGNITIVE COPING TECHNIQUES

A New Guide To Rational Living, by Albert Ellis and Robert Harper, Prentice-Hall, 1975.

Ellis, a psychologist, is widely known for his Rational Emotive Therapy (RET). Ellis has probably done more than any other psychologist to encourage self-help for people who are experiencing some form of distress in their lives. Ellis and Harper write in a clear, straightforward style, and their explanations of RET incorporate sound, practical, and easy-to-understand principles of behavior change. Their guide to RET rests on a basic premise: Irrational thinking causes unhappiness and negative feelings. Changes in negative feelings come about when we practice the kind of rational thinking Ellis and Harper outline in this book. It may not be the only way to happiness, but it's worth an honest try. *Available through Hazelden Educational Materials, order no. 6420.*

Own Your Own Life, by Gary Emery, Ph.D., New American Library, 1982.

Emery presents a workable and understandable approach to life's problems, based on a three step formula called ACT:
1. *A*ccept reality.
2. *C*hoose to be independent.
3. *T*ake action.

We can't control many things in life, says Emery, and it's important for us to recognize what we can control and what we can't. To a great extent, we can control how we think, feel, and act.

Emery outlines thinking errors and sets forth model plans of action that can be modified to fit individual circumstances. The ACT formula begins where the Serenity Prayer leaves off and helps us discover how to recognize and accept the things we can't change, gives us explicit methods for changing the things we can, and expands our wisdom to know the difference.

WARNER MEMORIAL LIBRARY
EASTERN COLLEGE
ST. DAVIDS, PA. 19087